德纳罗密档

——1877年中国海关筹印邮票之秘辛

赵　岳 译著

中华书局

谨以此书纪念海关大龙邮票发行 140 周年

目　录

德纳罗设计图稿

中文译本

目　录

档案英文

档案原本

目 录

附录　大龙邮品集萃

目　录

序　一

依据英国邮政的模式在中国发展一套现代邮政体系，是大清海关总税务司赫德爵士的众多愿景之一，加之中国也需要在海关的主理下发行自己的邮票。因而，赫德与是时英国最著名的邮票印刷商托马斯·德纳罗公司进行接洽便顺理成章。德纳罗致赫德的手绘样图（设计师的画稿）最终大约在 1877 年 6 月由中国海关伦敦办事处税务司金登干转呈，这是中国筹印首套邮票的初期设计，其重要性熟为众晓。

金登干和德纳罗之间就在英国或中国印制中国邮票问题的探讨此前不为世人所知。若在中国实施，则意味着机器、纸张及督管人员需由德纳罗提供。作为本书的资料来源，德纳罗档案为探究赫德构思的邮票问题提供了一个极佳的契机，从手绘样图的设计，到母模雕样的研究及彼时诸多的印制方法，细致入微，面面俱到，包括了油墨、胶水和打孔机，还有与之相关的安全问题（防伪对于邮票的印制而言尤为重要）、物料供应和运输事项。德纳罗在邮票印制方面拥有专业的技术和丰富的经验，从其同时极力推荐印制邮资信封也可见一斑。

此书标志着第一次有学者涉猎这份有关中国筹印首套邮票的档案。同时，该档案还是一份涉及邮票印制程序和步骤的技术性文件。

杰弗里·S.舒耐特

2018 年 6 月

Preface I

Among the goals of Sir Robert Hart, the Inspector General of the Chinese Imperial Maritime Customs, was the development of a modern postal system in China based on the model of the British post office. Coupled with this was the need for China to issue its own postage stamps under the auspices of the Customs service. Therefore, it was only logical that Hart approach Thomas De La Rue & Co., the foremost English printer of postage stamps at the time, in the first instance. The resultant hand painted essays (artist's drawings) submitted by De La Rue to Hart through the intermediary of the Chinese Customs Commissioner in London, J.D. Campbell, in June, 1877 were, in essence, the earlier designs for the first proposed stamp issue of China, and their importance as such has been universally recognised.

What has not been known previously is the correspondence between J.D. Campbell and De La Rue about the printing of stamps for China, either in England, or locally, which, for the latter case, would have meant that the machinery, paper and supervisory personnel would be supplied by De La Rue. The De La Rue Archives, upon which this book is based, provide a fascinating insight to the production of postage stamps as it relates to Hart's proposed issue, commencing with the hand painted designs and the study of their symbolism to the engraving of the master die, and the various methods of printing available at the time, with meticulous care and detail devoted to every aspect, including the inks, gum and perforating machinery, as well as the logistics relating to security (very important for postage stamps, especially so, in terms of deterring forgery), supply and transport. De La Rue's formidable expertise and experience in the printing of postage stamps is epitomised by the printer's strong recommendation to simultaneously print postal stationery envelopes.

This represents the first time that any researcher has consulted these archives concerning this first proposal for the issue of stamps for China. This original source also serves as a technical treatise for the processes and steps involved in printing postage stamps in general.

Jeffrey S. Schneider

June 2018

序 二

    将近二十年前，当我接受上海邮电管理局委托，为之撰写《中国邮票史》第一卷时，曾经根据当时可以见到的海关档案译文［主要是《清末天津海关邮政档案选编》《天津邮政史料》（第一辑）和《中国海关密档——赫德、金登干函电汇编（1874—1907）》[1]］，初步复原了 1877 至 1878 年海关筹印中国第一套邮票，即大龙邮票的相关史实。之所以说初步，是因为史实链条中还有不少缺环，赫德和德璀琳都读过的"德纳罗的长篇报告"[2] 即是其中之一，由于时间紧迫，条件有限，当时没有可能深入，只能留下遗憾。

    去年第四季度，赵岳告诉我在伦敦英国皇家邮政博物馆发现了

1　该书由中国第二历史档案馆和中国社科院近代史所合作编译，陈霞飞主编，全书共 9 册，中华书局 1990 年开始出版，至 1996 年出齐。此前，1975 年，美国哈佛大学东亚研究中心的费正清（J.K.Fairbank）教授主编出版了两卷本《总税务司在北京》（*THE I.G. IN PEKING: Letters of Robert Hart, Chinese Maritime Customs, 1868—1907*），但只有赫德的信函而无金登干的。台湾的邮史研究者曾据此研究中国近代邮政及邮票发行问题。有关赫德和金登干往来信函的收藏及流传，《中国海关密档》的前言有详细说明，可参阅。

2　陈霞飞主编：《中国海关密档——赫德、金登干函电汇编（1874—1907）》（第一卷），北京：中华书局 1990 年版，第 621 页。

一批档案，包括德纳罗公司 1877 年 6 月 8 日给清朝海关的专题信函及相关文件，准备翻译出版，问是否愿意帮忙做一点校订审读工作。我毫不犹豫，甚至有点急不可待地立即答应了。文史研究者的愉悦，莫过于从新资料中汲取新知识。想到能够从尘封已久的历史档案中了解未知的当年史实，怎么能不使人兴奋！

拜读德纳罗公司对清朝海关三个问题的回答，深感他们态度认真，叙述详尽，富有专业精神，当然背后也隐含商业推广之目的。对于当时的邮票制作，我以为至少有三个方面值得重视。

首先是印制工艺。19 世纪的印刷技术，欧美最为发达。德纳罗公司作为英国首屈一指的印制商，无疑站在技术前沿。其介绍涉及四种印刷工艺，即凹版、平版、压花和凸版，应该可以涵盖当时印制邮票所采用的最新技术。出人意料的是，德纳罗公司声言"我们已不再使用上述三种工艺，而是选择三十年前成功完成的改良型凸版邮票印刷工艺"，"这种工艺其实已经应用于我们印制的几乎所有邮票，从而使邮票免遭伪造，并且可以防止诈洗而被再次使用"。[1] 信函中没有描述此种工艺的细节，推测应为当年欧洲各国使用比较普遍的电铸工艺，即利用电解原理复制印版，具有复制精度高、复制方便等特点。日本于 19 世纪 70 年代引进此项技术用于邮票印制，如有兴趣，可参阅《中国邮票史》第二卷第三节。

1　参见本书第 121 页。

其次是邮票防伪。纸币及各种有价证券的防伪，一直是各国政府和印刷机构极为重视的。众所周知，主要出于防伪的考量，清朝国家邮政发行的伦敦版蟠龙邮票和民国初年发行的帆船邮票，都采用了雕刻凹版工艺，而大清银行发行的纸币和清朝度支部印刷局引进的印刷工艺，也都是雕刻凹版。德纳罗公司却告诉我们，凹版印制可以伪造，甚至便于作伪，并详细解释了如何伪造的技术过程。以我简陋的知识而言，此种作伪的复杂程度迥非常人可以操作，所以不能排除该公司故意贬低雕刻凹版的优点，推销自己印刷工艺的可能性。不过，详述邮票作伪手段对阅读过这份报告者有何影响，似可进一步探讨。以后，清朝国家邮政决定去日本印制邮票时，总税务司赫德和邮政总办葛显礼都特别强调了防伪问题。[1]

再次是印刷物资及设备的介绍，特别是油墨。报告比较详细地讲解了几种不同的邮票印制油墨，并附有票样说明，使人印象深刻。几年以后，海关主持印制小龙邮票，可能使用过带有水溶性颜料的油墨。此种油墨与德纳罗公司介绍的褪色油墨是否有关，似可作为进一步探讨的线索。1886 年，德璀琳在天津创办英文的《中国时报》，置办印刷设备，以后又引进英文打字铸排机，开办天津印刷公司。[2]

---

1 《费拉尔手稿——清代邮政邮票和明信片备忘录》，北京：人民邮电出版社 1991 年版，第 30-37 页。

2 万启盈编著：《中国近代印刷工业史》，上海：上海人民出版社 2012 年版，第 146 页。

此中机缘，又与德纳罗公司关于印刷机械的意见有无关系？凡此种种，似都可作为继续研究的课题。

为了准确理解德纳罗公司这批档案的内容，我查阅了几种关于中国近代印刷的史籍，由此对大龙邮票的子模复制有了新的想法。在撰写《中国邮票史》第一、二卷时，我曾经以为电铸印制工艺在20世纪初才传入中国，商务印书馆最先采用。现在知道，起码在1871年以前，上海的美华书馆已经使用该工艺复制印版，当年的报道称：

> 又有铜版，则非铜字排成，乃铸铜而成有字之全版。其法，始则以铅字为模，依书排字，继将排字覆印于蜡版之上，以黑铅粉涂蜡版上，以铜版与蜡版对置，置电气箱内，俄而电气化铜，蜡版吸铜而成铜版。铜版之字，坚光精妙，胜木版远矣。[1]

这种电气铸铜工艺，是否有可能被用于大龙邮票印制？

绵嘉义1905年"在造册处的铁柜里，发现有三方铜版"，"每方包含4枚每个独立的雕铜版模"，当时他认为"这些个独立的版模，

---

[1] 《美华书馆述略》，《教会新报》1871年第165期，转引自范慕韩主编《中国印刷近代史（初稿）》，北京：印刷工业出版社1995年版，第82页。

据说由当地工匠所雕刻"。[1] 现在我们已经知道，大龙邮票每种面值都有一个母模，再分别翻制子模，组成印版。大龙邮票的母模实物从未见报道，仅存世一件壹分银母模印样，而子模的复制工艺，由于资料欠缺，研究者解释不一，尚无共识。从现有资料大致可以断定，海关造册处印字房既不拥有母模，也不掌握复制子模的技术，所以当印模不断损坏时，只能通过减少全张枚数，甚至发行新邮票来解决问题。假设海关造册处需要委托外部机构制作大龙邮票印模，上述电铸工艺是一种可能的选择，因其技术特征隐隐相合。当然，在确凿的资料发现之前，这也只能是一种推测。

关于大龙邮票的设计者，在查阅史籍过程中似乎也有了新的线索。《北京工业志·印刷志》记述：

> 中国第一套邮票，是 1878 年 7 月由清海关邮政局在天津发行的"大龙邮票"，共 3 枚。是在清海关邮政局主持下，由中国老技师"样子李"承担设计绘制，以"九宫格"边框和五爪团花大龙为主图案，形成云龙戏珠图。[2]

1　绵嘉义：《海关首次大龙邮票重要资料》，《大龙邮票纪念专集——纪念大龙邮票发行 110 周年 1878—1988》，北京：中国集邮出版社 1988 年版，第 96 页。

2　陈升贵主编：《北京工业志·印刷志》，北京：中国科学技术出版社 2001 年版，第 262 页。

由于书中没有提供资料出处，让人无从知晓这种说法的来源，也就无法判断其价值。上引文中"清海关邮政局"的说法有误，当年并无此种机构。当年海关试办邮政，由德璀琳主持，其1877年在上海筹备巴黎世博会参展事宜，曾向赫德呈交"各种邮票图案"[1]。德璀琳应该雇有中国工匠，负责展品画样（即设计）和制作，很有可能他们中的一人，奉命提供了富有中国文化特色的邮票画稿。1937年出版的海关文件集有一条注释，称大龙邮票由一名中国画家设计。"中国老技师'样子李'"的说法，与此似乎出入不大。

赵岳这部译作，也使人想到在海外搜寻中国邮政和邮票资料的必要性。由于特殊的历史环境，记录中国近代重要人物和事件的文献，许多保留在海外的档案馆、博物馆和图书馆。譬如太平天国的印刷品，因清廷大批销毁，中国本土几乎荡然无存。20世纪30年代，学者萧一山和王重民相继公派出国考察，在大英博物馆东方部等处搜集到一批太平天国官书，回国后整理出版，使研究者得以目睹珍贵文献，从而大大推动了研究进展。当时人们以为，收藏在英国的太平天国文献差不多已搜罗殆尽。然而，1984年，学者王庆成还是在大英图书馆发现了太平天国刊刻的《天兄圣旨》和《天父圣旨》，对研究太平天国早期历史极为重要，而这两份文献，以前几乎

---

1 天津市档案馆、中国集邮出版社编，许和平、张俊桓译：《清末天津海关邮政档案选编》，北京：中国集邮出版社1988年版，第29页。

无人知晓。之所以说这些似乎不相干的话题，是希望在伦敦某个收藏单位的柜子里，还静静地躺着关于中国邮票的重要资料，等待我们去唤醒。

时值大龙邮票问世 140 周年，赵岳译著的《德纳罗密档——1877 年中国海关筹印邮票之秘辛》可以说是一份最好的生日礼物。希望更多的有心人关注这个领域，搜集更多的资料，特别是档案资料和历史文献，建构更为深入、具体和准确的邮史叙述框架。毕竟中国自己的邮票，最终还要由中国人自己完成其历史书写。

潘振平

2018 年 6 月

Preface II

Nearly twenty years ago, I was commissioned to author the First Volume of *The History of Chinese Postage Stamps*, as requested by the Shanghai Posts and Telecommunications Administration. Based on the monographs of the Customs' files, which might be located without too much difficulty at the time, namely the *Selected Archives of Tientsin Customs Post in Late Qing Dynasty, Postal History of Tientsin, Vol. I*, and *Archives of China's Imperial Maritime Customs: Confidential Correspondence between Robert Hart and James Duncan Campbell, 1874—1907*[1], I was preliminarily able to restore some of the relevant historical

---

1 The book was jointly compiled by the Second Historical Archives of China and Institute of Modern History of the Chinese Academy of Social Sciences. Both Chen Xiafei and Han Rongfang were the chief editors. This work consisted of 4 volumes, which was initially published in 1990 and completed by 1993. Dated back to 1975, John K. Fairbank of the Center for East Asian Research at Harvard University co-edited a two-volume publication, titled *THE I.G. IN PEKING: Letters of Robert Hart, Chinese Maritime Customs, 1868—1907*. However, only Hart's letters were included, without those of Campbell. Based on this book, the postal historians of Taiwan had studied subjects associated with the modern postal administration and stamp issuance policy of China. Concerning the collections and circulations of Hart and Campbell correspondence may be referred to the foreword of *Archives of China's Imperial Maritime Customs*, which should provide detailed description.

facts, as associated with the preparations carried out by the Customs between 1877 and 1878, for printing China's first set of stamps which have been called the Large Dragon stamps. I used the word "preliminarily" in my previous sentence because there were still some links missing in this long historical chain of facts. The "De La Rue's long report"[1], which should have been carefully read by Robert Hart and Gustav Detring, was surely one of the missing links. Under limited time and resources, I could then pursue no further but leave with regrets.

In the fourth quarter of last year, Zhao Yue informed me that he had discovered a batch of documents at the Postal Museum, London, which included a De La Rue's letter on specific topics, dated June 8, 1877, addressed to the Maritime Customs of Qing, along with other related papers. He would have these documents translated and then published. Furthermore, he asked me whether I might help reviewing the monograph. Without the slightest hesitation, I, in fact, could scarcely wait to promise. There is nothing more to please the researchers in literary and history than to furnish them with newly discovered documents for acquiring further knowledge. I just felt all excited to think of learning the unknown historical facts by unveiling the dust sealed archives.

After reading the replies of Thomas De La Rue & Co. to the three questions raised by the Imperial Customs of Qing, I felt deeply

---

1 Chen Xiafei and Han Rongfang chief ed., *Archives of China's Imperial Maritime Customs: Confidential Correspondence between Robert Hart and James Duncan Campbell, 1874—1907*, Vol. I, p.314, 1990, Foreign Languages Press, Beijing.

that their attitudes were prudent; their descriptions were detailed and they possessed professional consciousness. Lastly, but surely, the replies also implied the intention of promoting their core business. As for the stamp production processes practiced in 1870s, I consider there should be at least three aspects worthy of attention.

The first is the printing process. In the nineteenth century, the printing technology was very well developed in the Occident. As the most renowned printing house in Great Britain, Thomas De La Rue & Co. undoubtedly should be standing at the leading edge of technology. The Company provided information on four different systems, namely the intaglio, lithographic, embossing and surface printing processes. These four processes should have represented the then mainstream technologies employed for printing stamps. Unexpectedly, De La Rue stated the followings, "all these considerations have led us to discard the three processes which we have discussed above in favour of the improved surface stamp printing process which we succeeded in perfecting some thirty years ago, ...This process is in fact now employed for almost all the stamps which we manufacture, and it enables us to produce stamps which are secure against forgery and are proof against being fraudulently cleaned and used a second time."[1] Nonetheless, the details of the surface printing process were not clearly described in the letter. This might be due to the electrotyping process was more widely used in Europe during the period, which could replicate the printing plates by means of electrolysis. Moreover, the characteristic feature of electrotyping process

---

1 Refer to p.198 of this book.

was to produce replicas with high precision conveniently. In 1870s, Japan introduced the technology to facilitate the stamp production. For those who are interested, please refer to Section 3 in the Volume II of *The History of Chinese Postage Stamps*.

The second is the anti-forgery of stamps. The anti-counterfeiting of banknotes and negotiable securities have been paid tremendous attentions by governments and printing organizations globally. As we may have known, the "Coiling Dragon" and "Junk" Issues were released by the Chinese Imperial Post and Republican Post, respectively. Both Issues were produced in London, using the intaglio printing process, as well as taking anti-forgery into chief consideration. The banknotes of the Ta-Ching Government Bank were printed by the intaglio process, and the printing process imported by the Printing Bureau of the Imperial Department of Treasury was intaglio, as well. Ironically, De La Rue informed us that stamps printed by the intaglio process might be counterfeited or even altered easily. Furthermore, the counterfeiting and fraudulent processes were explained in excessive details. To my humble knowledge, I must point out the level of complexity involved in counterfeiting process of this sort just could not be manipulated by normal human beings. Hence, we may not rule out the possibility that De La Rue was trying to promote its own printing process by deliberately downgrading the advantages of intaglio, instead. On the other hand, the subsequent influence on the Imperial Customs officials, after reading this detailed report on the forgery means, may likely be raised for further discussions. In the latter days, the Inspector General Robert Hart and Chief Commissioner Henry C.J. Kopsch indeed placed special emphases on the subject of anti-forgery[1], as the Chinese Imperial Post decided to have one of the stamp issues printed in Japan.

The last is the introduction of printing materials, especially the printing inks, and equipment. The De La Rue's report contained comprehensive descriptions on a few types of inks used for stamp printing, with the illustrations of related specimens, and that was impressive. Some years later, the Imperial Customs Post presided over the production of the Small Dragon Issue in which the printing inks comprising of water soluble pigments might have been employed. Whether this kind of inks was, in any manner, related to the fugitive inks, as strongly recommended by De La Rue, would likely to be the clue for further study. In 1886, Gustav Detring started to acquire printing equipment and then founded the English newspaper, *The Chinese Times*, in Tianjin. He later imported the English typing and composing machine for setting up the Tientsin Printing Company.[2] Was there any possible correlation between his career opportunities and De La Rue's opinions on printing machineries? All in all, this may again be treated as a topic for further research.

To thoroughly understand the contents of De La Rue's Archives, I have consulted a few historical records on modern Chinese printing. Subsequently, this leads to the formation of a new concept

---

1　*Proposed Stamps, etc. & Postcards for the Imperial Chinese Post Memos*, pp.30-37, 1991, Posts & Telecom Press, Beijing.
2　Wan Qiying ed., *The History of Modern Printing Industry in China*, p.146, 2012, Shanghai People's Publishing House, Shanghai.

on cliché replication for the Large Dragon stamps. When I was writing the Volumes I and II of *The History of Chinese Postage Stamps*, I considered the electrotyping technology was introduced to China in the early twentieth century, and the Commercial Press ought to be the first printing house to adopt the process. Now I know, the American Presbyterian Mission Press of Shanghai had employed the process to replicate its printing plates at least before 1871. For this occasion, it was reported as follows:

> *There was this copper printing plate which was not formed by arranging words made of copper. All words were actually casted to yield one complete copper printing plate. The process was started by using words made of lead as dies. These cubic dies of lead were arranged as required by the typesetting, which were then impressed on the surface of a wax plate. The stencil was dusted by the black lead powders, which was positioned face-to-face with a copper plate, and both were immersed in the electrolysis trough. The copper was electrified and absorbed by the wax plate which in turn formed the copper printing plate. The words appeared on the copper plate were solid and exquisite and far better than those on the wooden plates.*[1]

---

1 *A Review on the American Presbyterian Mission Press*, *The Church News*, No. 165, 1871. Referred from Fan Muhan ed., *The Modern History of Printing in China, First Draft*, p.82, 1995, The Printing Industry Publishing House, Beijing.

Could there be a possibility that the same electrotyping process was used for producing the Large Dragon stamps?

In 1905, Juan Mencarini "discovered three blocks of copper dies in a metal cabinet at the Statistical Department, ….Each block consisted of four individual pieces of copper die." Allegedly, "these individual copper dies were engraved by local craftsmen."[1] We should have known by now, each denomination of the Large Dragon Issue had its own master die which was replicated to produce the clichés subsequently. Then, the clichés were arranged to form the printing plate. However, the master dies of the Large Dragons have never been reported, and a proof of the One-Candarin is the only item known to exist. Due to the lack of related documents, the researchers have been expressing different opinions on the replication process adopted for producing the clichés, and the consensus is yet to be reached. According to the existing literatures, we may conclude the Printing Office of Statistical Department had neither the master dies nor the skill for replicating the clichés. Therefore, if the clichés were constantly damaged, the problem could seemingly be solved by reducing the number of stamps in a full sheet or even by releasing new issues. By assuming the Statistical Department did need to entrust the production of dies of the Large Dragons to some external organizations, then, the employment of electrotyping process, as mentioned previously, might stand for a possible choice, as

---

1 Juan Mencarini, *Important Information on the First Stamps, the Large Dragons, of the Customs*, p.96, *The Large Dragons*, 1988, China Philatelic Publishing House, Beijing.

the technical characteristics of the process shared a few similarities with the Large Dragons. Surely, this is only a conjecture before the discovery of some solid evidences.

After going through some historical records, I may also have a new clue with regard to the designer of the Large Dragons. It was stated in *The Printing Chronicles* of *The Beijing Industrial Chronicles*:

> *The first set of Chinese stamps were the Large Dragons which were issued in Tianjin by the Chinese Imperial Customs Post Office1 in July of 1878. The task of designing and drawing this set of three stamps, under the auspices of the Chinese Imperial Customs Post Office, was undertaken by an aged Chinese craftsman, nicknamed "Limner Li". He used the "nine-rectangle-grid" to establish the border frames, along with an Ipomoea Cairica, composing the auspicious scene of a dragon playing with a pearl in cloud, as the central design.[2]*

As the Chronicles do not furnish the origin of this piece of information, we thus are in no manners to evaluate its importance. However, the citations of "Chinese Imperial Customs Post Office" in the above statement were mistakenly presented, and there was,

---

1 The original Chinese text was "清海关邮政局", or "Chinese Imperial Customs Post Office", which was not the official name.

2 Chen Shenggui ed., *The Printing Chronicles* of *The Beijing Industrial Chronicles*, p.262, 2001, China Science and Technology Press, Beijing.

in fact, no such organization with the title during the period. The postal service initially offered by the Imperial Customs and overseen by Detring was only a trial operation. In 1877, Detring was busy preparing for China's participation in the Exposition Universelle de Paris. He submitted "various sketches of postage stamps "[1] to Hart. This might also imply Detring should have hired Chinese craftsmen to handle the designs and productions of the Chinese exhibits, and one of the craftsmen could probably be responsible for providing stamp design sketches with distinguishing Chinese cultural features. There was an annotation in a book, published in 1937, on a collection of Customs documents, which claimed the Large Dragon stamps were designed by a Chinese painter. There seemed to be little discrepancy between the Chinese painter and an aged Chinese craftsman, known as "Limner Li".

This volume of translated works by Zhao Yue reminds us of the essentiality of searching overseas for related documents on Chinese Post and its issued stamps. Due to our special historical circumstances, quite a few literatures, recording the important figures and events of modern time China, are presently kept in the archives, museums and libraries abroad. As an example, the printed matters of the Taiping Heavenly Kingdom of Great Peace were largely destroyed by the Qing Government, and there was almost nothing left on the Chinese soil. In the 30s of 20th century, two Chinese

---

1 Tianjin Archives and China Philatelic Publishing House ed., Xu Heping and Zhang Junhuan trans., *Selected Archives of Tientsin Customs Post in Late Qing Dynasty*, p.44, 1988, China Philatelic Publishing House, Beijing.

scholars, Xiao Yishan and Wang Chongmin, were successively sent overseas by the government for conducting a survey. They were able to collect a handsome amount of the official publications of Taiping Heavenly Kingdom from the Department of Asia at British Museum. After returning to China, they reorganized the finds and had them published. This enabled the researchers to read and study these invaluable literatures and, hence, greatly promoted the progresses of researches in the related areas. Just about everyone thought the literatures related to the Taiping Heavenly Kingdom should have been drained to the limit in Great Britain. However, another Chinese scholar, Wang Qingcheng, unexpectedly found the inscribed *Decree of Heavenly Father* and *Decree of Heavenly Brother* of the Taiping Heavenly Kingdom at the British Library in 1984. These were extremely important to researchers who studied the early history of Taiping Heavenly Kingdom. Before the discovery of these two scarce items, hardly anybody had knowledge of their existences. To mention these seemingly unrelated topics, I have this wishful thinking that some important documents, concerning the Chinese postage stamps, might still be lying quietly inside the cabinets of some organizations in London and are waiting for us to wake them up to rewrite the history.

The year of 2018 marks the 140th anniversary for the birth of the Large Dragons. *The De La Rue Archives for China, 1877*, translated and written by Zhao Yue, may be regarded as the best birthday present ever. I hope more conscientious people might pay attentions to this field by collecting more information, especially documentary files and historical literatures, and accumulating

more in-depth knowledge to construct some specific and precise
frameworks for the narrative of postal history. After all, these are
our own Chinese stamps, and their history should eventually be
written on our own.

Pan Zhenping

June 2018

导　言

1877年的中国海关与英国德纳罗

作为中国海关发行的第一套邮票，大龙邮票以其迥殊的历史地位备受各界眷注，其发行背景和发行时间一直广为学者热议。由于多次印刷，大龙邮票版式复杂，实寄信封存世罕见，邮学价值重大，也成为中国古典邮票集藏家醉心爱赏的对象。

1925 年，周今觉在《邮乘》上发表文章，对大龙邮票的设计、面值、刷色、发行数量和版式等问题作出了探索性的研究。20 世纪 40 年代，陈志川和孙君毅等先后在《国粹邮刊》《邮典》《新光邮票杂志》和《邮友》等刊物上发表文章，对大龙邮票进行深一步研讨。1949 年 3 月，大卫德爵士（Sir Percival David）在《伦敦集邮家》第 58 卷第 676 期上撰写了《中国第一套邮票的图稿、试样和印样》，详细介绍了与大龙邮票相关的画稿、设计图稿以及各种母模、子模试样和印样。1978 年，在大龙邮票发行一百周年之际，艾尔兰（Philip W. Ireland）出版了著名的《大龙邮票》（*CHINA——The*

Large Dragons 1878—1885），全面系统介绍了中国大龙邮票的发行背景、过程以及邮票的子模和版式。

1980 年，孙志平在当年第 3 期《集邮》杂志上发表的《大龙邮票发行日期之我见》，激起学界广泛而热烈的反响，多位集邮家和海关史研究人员先后撰文叙谈感想，掀起了以大龙邮票发行时间和背景为主题的邮学大讨论，时间长达五年之久。此次众议相商的结果，让扑朔迷离的大龙邮票发行时间逐渐理清了头绪，以可靠的档案确立了"七月说"，这是 1949 年以后中国集邮界对大龙邮票研究最为重要的贡献。

1988 年，天津市档案馆和中国集邮出版社合编的《清末天津海关邮政档案选编》，以及 1990 至 1995 年中国社会科学院近代史研究所陈霞飞主编的《中国海关密档——赫德、金登干函电汇编（1874—1907）》（第一卷至第九卷），为研究大龙邮票的发行背景提供了重要的一手史籍。1993 和 1997 年，台湾黄建斌编撰的《大龙邮票集锦 1878—1885》和《大龙信封存世考》公开出版，这两本专著已成为方今大龙邮票收集与研究的重要工具书。

自大龙邮票发行伊始，众多海内外邮学家为大龙邮票的集藏付出了大量的心血。其中较为突出的有：阿格纽（John A. Agnew）、大卫德爵士、施塔少校（Major James Starr）、高达医生（Dr. Warren G. Kauder）、吉尔伯特（G. Gilbert）、艾尔兰、霍克（Paul P. Hock）、水原明窗（Meiso Mizuhara）、贝克曼夫妇（Anna-Lisa and Sven-Eric

Beckeman）、奥尔森夫妇（Jane and Dan Sten Olsson）、周今觉、郭植芳、陈湘涛、黄天湧、黄建斌、吴乐园、林文琰和李镜禹等。吉尔伯特、李忠厚（Robert C.H. Lee）、陈湘涛、霍克和贝克曼等还通过对存世实物的梳理、分类，总结归纳了大龙邮票的众多版式特征。

回看大龙邮票一百多年来的研究成果，著作颇丰，成绩斐然，但仍有不少谜团有待破解，特别是邮票发行的初始，即 1876 至 1878 年这段时期，由于资料的散失，形成了一些学术空白和认知模糊。此外，在最近二十年，没有挖掘出更多的新资料，学界在大龙邮票的研究上未能取得实质性的突破和进展。

2017 年 10 月下旬，为参与中国邮政邮票博物馆与中国海关博物馆联合举行"大龙邮票发行 140 周年纪念"学术征文活动，笔者专程前往伦敦，徜徉于大英图书馆、英国邮政博物馆、雷丁大学图书馆和英国皇家集邮协会资料室，在海量的资料中寻找 140 年前与中国海关筹印邮票相关的蛛丝马迹。经过不懈的努力，发掘了颇多有用的资料，尤其是 1877 年德纳罗公司中国档案，这也就成了本书辑集出版的重要机缘。

1877 年中国海关与英国德纳罗的渊源伊始

为了效仿西方在中国开办现代邮政业务，海关总税务司赫德（Robert Hart）集思广益，要求各地的海关税务司对此建言献策，根据《中国邮票史》推测,时间应"不会晚于 1876 年年底之前"[1]。现有资料中，发现最早与海关邮票发行问题相关的档案是 1877 年 3 月 5 日德璀琳（Gustav Detring）致金登干（James Duncan Campbell）函[2]。在这份保存在天津档案馆的资料中，时任东海关（烟台）税务司的德璀琳[3]，就总税务司的拟题向中国海关伦敦办事处税务司金登干致函征询：

　　1. 在英国印制一百万枚邮票，开销几何？

　　2. 采购机器设备和纸张在中国每周印制一百万枚邮票，耗资几许？

　　3. 如基本辅助劳力皆在中国就地雇佣，每周印制一百万枚邮票，英国雇员每月所需的用度几多？[4]

　　德璀琳恳请金登干迅疾作出回复，并央浼帮助觅寻"最新版本的英国和法国邮政法规"以及"这两个国家现有的邮政空白表格"[5]。自此，中国海关在伦敦筹印邮票的系列探索通过金登干正式展开，

1　中华人民共和国信息产业部《中国邮票史》编审委员会编：《中国邮票史》（第一卷），北京：商务印书馆 1999 年版，第 101 页。
2　天津市档案馆、中国集邮出版社编，许和平、张俊桓译：《清末天津海关邮政档案选编》，北京：中国集邮出版社 1988 年版，第 21-22 页。
3　德璀琳于 1877 年底调任津海关（天津）税务司。
4　天津市档案馆、中国集邮出版社编，许和平、张俊桓译：《清末天津海关邮政档案选编》，北京：中国集邮出版社 1988 年版，第 21 页。根据第 23-25 页的原文，译文有修改。
5　同上，第 21-22 页。

1877 也就成了中国邮票史上一个格外特殊的年光。为践诺德璀琳的询函所求，金登干在伦敦与技术雄厚、历史悠长的印刷公司德纳罗进行接洽，这就是后来其致赫德的书信与电报中不断地谈及的"De La Rue"。有关金登干与德纳罗公司的接触经过，在过往 140 年的各类史籍之中，虽然有过一些提及，但并没有与之直接相关的资料，这使得中国海关早期在伦敦筹印邮票的活动蒙披了一些朦胧的色彩。此次我们发现，写有上述三个问题的询函粘贴在德纳罗公司 1877 年中国档案的第一页，询函左下角贴有金登干的名片，右上角标注的时间为 1877 年 5 月 1 日。三个问题的英文与天津市档案馆所存资料除了时间之外，不差丝毫。询函没有具名，从笔迹分析，异于德璀琳与金登干所书，应为第三人誊抄。每条问题的后面均有答案，用铅笔书写：

1. 50-60 英镑

2. 设想而已

3. 将会出具详尽报告

对于"采购机器设备和纸张在中国印制邮票"这一问题，德纳罗公司认为好似离奇夜谭，无法兑现。之所以如此武断，不仅出于商业角度，亦是对彼时中国相关技术力量的偏隅之见。5 月 5 日，金登干在给赫德的 161 号电报中，如实转达："致德璀琳：关于邮票的第一个问题，约需 50-60 镑；第二、三两个问题，认为无法实现，一切细节两星期后可完成。"[1]

德璀琳致金登干的征询原原本本地存现于德纳罗 1877 中国档案的第一页，足以说明双方的交往源自赫德创设邮政的设想，德纳罗档案也就成了相关活动的具体佐证。

1877 年中国海关与英国德纳罗的合作进程

围绕 1877 年 5 月 1 日金登干转询的三个问题，德纳罗公司步入了以邮票的设计、印制为主题的具体落实进程。关于这个进程的推进，在《中国海关密档——赫德、金登干函电汇编（1874—1907）》中有一些线索。下面我们把该书的相关内容与此次新发现的档案，以时间为序作一个串并，以便更好地解读这段历史。

5 月 5 日，也就是金登干与德纳罗公司正式接触后的第四天，金登干把初步答案通过给赫德的电报转告给了德璀琳，金登干之所以没有直接回复，而是在给赫德的电报中顺带提及，明确表明金登干不希望此事的接洽绕过顶头上司，同时也在暗示，所有后继行动，均应得到赫德的首肯方可顺利推进。5 月 11 日，金登干再次向赫德

---

1 陈霞飞主编：《中国海关密档——赫德、金登干函电汇编（1874—1907）》（第八卷），北京：中华书局 1995 年版，第 115 页。

呈报，说德璀琳需要的报告最快要下周才能备妥，而且特别提到当时的九江税务司葛显礼（H. Kopsch）也在为"设法筹划邮政系统"忙活不已[1]。

5 月 22 日和 23 日，金登干接连两次致函德纳罗公司。22 日，为助于邮票的设计，金登干给德纳罗公司寄去了"来自北京的两幅画稿"，并提供了一幅"龙"图作为参考。23 日，金登干又就 22 日所提供的画稿中什么是"阴阳"特别作出说明。

6 月 8 日，德纳罗公司出具了一份长达 42 页的机密报告。该报告在档案中的原始日期 6 月 8 日用铅笔划去，并在左侧注明："金登干先生将此日期修改为 18 日，见他 1877 年 6 月 29 日的信函。"之所以要求德纳罗公司修改报告的时间，应该与金登干没有在原先计划的时间内完成报告相关。6 月 22 日，金登干在给赫德的信中又提及德璀琳的请托："我正在就德璀琳两个多月以前委托我的关于邮政事务一事给你缮写一份公文；我希望这份资料会有用处。"[2] 信中所说的公文，应该与德纳罗公司 6 月 8 日的报告相干。

7 月 5 日和 6 日两天，德纳罗和金登干之间各自寄发了两份信函，内容主要涉及金登干提交的订货单。这些订货单共计 6 份，没有注明日期，所采购的物资是平版印刷机、打孔机、油墨、纸张、胶水

1　陈霞飞主编：《中国海关密档——赫德、金登干函电汇编（1874—1907）》（第一卷），北京：中华书局 1990 年版，第 535-536 页。
2　同上，第 558 页。

和信件磅秤。金登干希望德纳罗公司能够配合完成订货单的审核，以便倘若总税务司决定在中国印制邮票时能得以方便，而德纳罗公司则反复强调，订货单所采购的物资不能满足邮票的印制，同时明确表示，从邮票的防伪等角度考虑，找德纳罗来印制邮票是中国海关的不二之选。

根据档案分析，德纳罗公司收到这些订货单的时间应该为7月2日。两天后，也就是7月4日，双方还就这些订单的落实有过一次晤谈。见面之后，金登干电报赫德："邮政订货单无法实施，机器、纸张和油墨皆不适用，详细报告已于6月22日寄出。您如立即寄来与上次英国邮票大小类似的设计稿，收我汇报后再作电报指示，各种邮票可以在十周后送抵这里（伦敦）交货，价格为每百万枚55镑。先在这里印制，可保证有熟练的生产经验，节省时间并确保防伪——日后再向中国转产。"[1] 这份电报的内容，金登干7月5日也给德纳罗转抄了一份。对比这两份电报的英文原文，内容基本一致，但稍有差别，其中最主要的一点就是给赫德的电报中说印制每百万枚邮票的价格为"55"镑，而在给德纳罗公司的电报副本中却变成了"54"，这个有趣的现象如果非笔误所致，那深层次的原因确实值得思考，有兴趣的朋友可以参阅《中国海关密档——赫德、金登干函电汇编

---

1 陈霞飞主编：《中国海关密档——赫德、金登干函电汇编（1874—1907）》（第八卷），北京：中华书局1995年版，第120页。译文有修改。

（1874—1907）》（第一卷）第 632-635 页 A/144 号信函有关佣金的章节，或可得到些许启示。而另一点重要不同就是电报中所提及的"与上次英国邮票大小类似的设计稿"在给德纳罗公司的副本中却改成了"每种邮票的设计"，这个所谓的"与上次英国邮票大小类似的设计稿"，目前没有发现相关资料，但有一点可以肯定，那就是金登干不想这件事情让德纳罗公司所知晓。

　　7 月 6 日，金登干为订货单之事致函赫德："德璀琳请印制邮票，使我感到为难。即使我给他订货，也要三四个月才能准备好。无法如我原来所愿，把我必须匆匆赶写的那封公函抄件寄给德璀琳。"[1]7 月 13 日，金登干再次为订货单致函："关于邮票事公文，现在没有什么可补充说明。延误无疑使您失望。不过，即使我向采购单上开列的那些公司订货，大概也要六个月后才能全部寄到上海，——留出承包商的耽搁发生事故等等而拖延的时间。若找德纳罗公司代为印制，则不仅可以很好地按订货单办事，而且可以节省时间和费用。如果您决定在这里开始印制，那么，也许最好把齿孔机运送到中国去，这样，邮票要在中国经过最后一道工序——并经检验——以后才能发行。"[2]

1　陈霞飞主编：《中国海关密档——赫德、金登干函电汇编（1874—1907）》（第一卷），北京：中华书局 1990 年版，第 563 页。
2　同上，第 564 页。

上述两封信清晰表明，德纳罗档案中的那六份订单是应德璀琳的要求所为，而且德璀琳在 5 月份为了买这批物资，曾向中国海关伦敦办事处汇款 1000 英镑[1]。比照 7 月 4 日的电报内容，从具体的落实时间而言，在德纳罗订制邮票，大概需时十周，也就是两个半月左右。而如果在中国印制，金登干 7 月 6 日的信中说买原料及设备的时间就需要三四个月，二者如何抉择如何取舍，金登干没有明言。而 7 月 13 日的信中金登干非常直白地道出了找德纳罗印制可以节省人力物力，说不算上供货商的耽搁，到上海至少六个月。所以，金登干看似只在汇报事情进展，但其倾向无可遮掩。当然，赫德也应心知肚明。

7 月 20 日，金登干致函赫德："您 6 月 2 日的 Z/6 号函已收到，但是您的 Z/5 号函必定已在'湄公'号轮船上丢失了。此外，我担心德璀琳说明邮政问题的备忘录也一同丢失了。"[2] 其实，金登干在 7 月 5 日早已向德纳罗告知轮船失事一事。

10 月 25 日，赫德致金登干："非常感谢德纳罗的长篇报告。我们将在他那里制作我们的邮票，但是我不想仓促地听从德璀琳过于

---

1 天津市档案馆、中国集邮出版社编，许和平、张俊桓译：《清末天津海关邮政档案选编》，北京：中国集邮出版社 1988 年版，第 165 页。

2 陈霞飞主编：《中国海关密档——赫德、金登干函电汇编（1874—1907）》（第一卷），北京：中华书局 1990 年版，第 569 页。

乐观的主张。一定要首先站稳我的脚跟，然后再推进这项业务。"[1]赫德所提到的"长篇报告"应该就是德纳罗公司 6 月 8 日的机密报告，虽然赫德表示会在德纳罗公司制作邮票，但在后来两个多月里，并没有给予金登干下一步行动的明确指示。

1877 年 12 月中旬，中国海关伦敦办事处曾与德纳罗之间就标的为"1000 份深绿色硬布封面"的订货有过一次合作，这些"深绿色硬布封面"是帛黎翻译的法文版《圣谕广训》的精致硬装封面。从档案保存的材料看，此次合作因时间延至 1878 年，后继细节暂不知晓，但目前保存在中国国家图书馆、大英图书馆等地的 1879 年法文版《圣谕广训》应该就是这次合作的成果。为什么在筹印邮票的过程中穿插进这次采购，是否是金登干在等候赫德指示期间为稳住德纳罗的权宜之举，与最终邮票的印制没有能合作成功是否相关，谜底暂无法揭晓。

没有得到赫德明确指示的金登干，1878 年 1 月 4 日电报赫德："德璀琳寄来邮票订货单，我是否应代他订货？"[2]发出电报的金登干，又在同一天给赫德去信（A/147 号）："德纳罗先生频频询问我是否已获悉您对他的备忘录有什么意见。我已向他转达了您在这件事情

---

1 陈霞飞主编：《中国海关密档——赫德、金登干函电汇编（1874—1907）》（第一卷），北京：中华书局 1990 年版，第 621 页。
2 同上（第八卷），1995 年版，第 141 页。

上对他表示的谢意。"[1] 同一天的另外一封信（A/148号）中，金登干还向赫德汇报了德璀琳看过德纳罗报告后的意见，说德璀琳专门就邮票问题给他发函："海关需用的几种面值业经总税务司审阅择定。图案当然应缩小到普通邮票的尺寸。图案所选用的色彩，也已在附件中详细说明。"[2] 此函另附四种邮票的设计图案。从1877年10月底收到德纳罗的报告，到1878年1月初金登干发电催办，赫德一直没有对何时启动明确表态，因此金登干在信中拿德璀琳来说事，其急不可耐的念头已然落于笔端。心虚必然多话，为自证清白，亦担心赫德误解，信中金登干最后还是赘上了一笔，以示忠心不二："附件是'商请（中国海关）驻伦敦办事处主任经办定制的邮票订货单'一纸。经查阅，您在A/46号函件中曾明示，您一定要首先站稳脚跟、然后再图推进邮政业务等语。奉此，在接到您准予照办的指示以前，暂缓订制。"[3]

2月24日，赫德就金登干1月4日的电报询问回复金登干："请推迟发出邮票订单。"[4] 中国海关在伦敦筹印邮票以及中国海关与德纳罗的合作就此作罢。

有关德璀琳从中国寄发的四种邮票设计图案，根据文件记载，

---

1 陈霞飞主编：《中国海关密档——赫德、金登干函电汇编（1874—1907）》（第二卷），北京：中华书局1990年版，第3页。

2 同上，第4页。

3 同上，第4-5页。

4 同上（第八卷），1995年版，第148页。译文有修改。

这些图案实际上是 1877 年 5 月份提交并获得了批准，11 月份寄给了伦敦的金登干[1]，图案分别为："蹲伏的龙"、"凤凰"、"背负万年青的大象"和"宝塔"[2]。从资料上所表述的图案内容看，"蹲伏的龙"、"背负万年青的大象"和"宝塔"这三幅图稿应该就是后来保存在水原明窗邮集的三种试样，"蹲伏的龙"实际上也就是后来的大龙邮票的图案，所谓的"蹲伏"只不过是对云龙盘卷形态的理解和表述。为什么在收到英国方面的详细报告及设计方案，德璀琳也向英国寄出了中方的设计图稿后，赫德会突然叫停了与德纳罗的合作进程，个中原委，有待进一步研究。

1877 年德纳罗为中国海关设计的图稿

德纳罗 1877 年 6 月 8 日的报告涉及德纳罗印刷技术的核心概要，因此标注了"机密"字样。考虑当时的中国国情及各种印刷工艺的优劣与适用，报告详尽地解释了各种印刷工艺的技术细节，向中国海关提出了具体建议，原文共计 42 页。为让当时远在中国的决策者能够直观地了解各种工艺的印制效果，德纳罗在报告后附录了 12 份附件，从 A 至 L，具体见下表：

1　天津市档案馆、中国集邮出版社编，许和平、张俊桓译：《清末天津海关邮政档案选编》，北京：中国集邮出版社 1988 年版，第 164-165 页。
2　杜圣余：《大龙邮票的图稿、试印样票》，《集邮》1988 年第 10 期，第 20 页。

附件	附 件 内 容
附件 A	用四种印刷工艺印制的邮票票样
附件 B	"易褪色"油墨和普通油墨印制的邮票在溶剂作用下的不同反应
附件 C	销戳机照片和销戳示样
附件 D	销戳示样和含地名、日期的邮戳草图
附件 E	三种用"双褪色"油墨所印制的票样
附件 F	水印邮票纸和背胶邮票纸
附件 G	为英国政府印制的信封
附件 H	为印度印制的两个品种或面值的信封样品
附件 I	为中国海关设计的邮资信封图稿以及两种面值的压印邮资符图稿
附件 J	为中国海关设计的纸张水印图稿和两种邮票图稿
附件 K	12 分香港邮票四分之一全张票样
附件 L	"印花纸"样张

上述附件的原件没有随报告一同保存在德纳罗 1877 年的档案之中，档案中只留存一份附件 I 的复印件。

附件 J 曾在 1955 年"德纳罗公司印制邮票一百周年展览"中公开展出，当时展览资料的两份胶卷目前分存于英国皇家邮政博物馆和英国斯宾客（Spink）拍卖公司。展页的上方标注："1877 年，我们与中国海关税务司金登干先生接洽，他来自大清帝国海关总税务司署伦敦办事处，我们向他提交了一份有关印刷邮票的方案。附件 J 于 1877 年 6 月 18 日提交。"1958 年英国皇家集邮协会出版的《德纳罗英国及海外邮票史（1855—1901）》(The DE LA RUE HISTORY of BRITISH & FOREIGN POSTAGE STAMPS, 1855 to 1901) 刊载了附件 J 中的邮票设计图稿[1]。2014 年英国皇家集邮协会出版的《德纳罗藏集》(The De La Rue Collection) 一书中登载了 1955 年附件 J 的展页[2]。

此外，附件 A1955 年也曾随同附件 J 一起公开展出，并在《德纳罗藏集》中出版[3]。1955 年展出时，德纳罗公司特意在附件 A 的下方展示一套中国海关 1878 年发行的大龙邮票，以反映 1877 年其为中国海关筹印邮票时所作出的探索和努力。

附件 I 和附件 J 包括：1. 邮资信封图稿；2. 圆和椭圆两种邮资信封邮资符图稿；3. 太极阴阳图水印图稿；4. 横向和竖向长方形邮票图稿，两类各三枚。附件 I 在邮资信封图稿的上方标注："推荐给中国之邮资信封样品，一只展示正面，另一只为背面。"邮资信封邮资符图稿的上方标注："为上面邮资信封推荐的压印邮资符图稿。"附

---

1 John Easton, The DE LA RUE HISTORY of BRITISH & FOREIGN POSTAGE STAMPS, 1855 to 1901, plate48, 1958, Faber and Faber, London.

2 Frank Walton, The De La Rue Collection, p.2567, 2014, The Royal Philatelic Society, London.

3 同上 , p.2566.

件 J 在太极阴阳水印图稿上方标注："推荐给中国邮票所用纸张的水印图稿。"在邮票设计稿的上方标注："推荐给中国邮票之备选图稿，其面值系属假设。"附件 J 的最下方还粘贴了两枚印样，上方标注："中心为动物或鸟类的背胶邮票的雕刻印样。"

附件 I 中的两种邮资符图稿，圆形面值为"一分"，红色；椭圆面值为"二分"，绿色。附件 J 分为横、竖两类，每类 3 种面值，分别为"一分"、"二分"和"五分"，一分面值红色，二分面值绿色，五分面值黄色。之所以选用这些颜色，其实在上面介绍的德纳罗档案第一页文件的下方有用铅笔书写的五种颜色及相关注释：

黄色	御用之色
红色和粉色	欣悦
蓝色	哀伤
绿色	欣悦
棕色	哀伤

德纳罗在设计时选用了黄色、红色和绿色，其中"御用之色"的黄色用于最高面值。在后来大龙邮票印制时，也采用了这三种颜色，只不过大龙一分银为绿色，三分银为红色，五分银为黄色，这是一种巧合，还是与德纳罗的建议相关，暂无定论。

"赫德画稿"与"德纳罗设计稿"之间的关系

　　关于北京寄来的画稿，在 1877 年 5 月 22 日金登干致德纳罗函的最后特别注明："方案拟妥，烦将两张小画稿归还。"23 日的信函中再次指出："昨天寄奉贵司的两张小画稿中，各有一个悬浮在中的球体，即所谓'阴阳'。"可以看出，北京的画稿共计两张，图幅不大，图案中间各有一个"阴阳"符号。这两份画稿由于金登干要求退还，故而没有保存在德纳罗的档案中。那么画稿的庐山真面目究竟何样？由此联想到源自赫德遗集的"双龙戏珠"和"龙凤戏珠"画稿[1]（以下简称"赫德画稿"）。长期以来，由于没有相关资料佐证，对于"赫德画稿"的真实用途众说纷纭，曾有学者认为，"赫德画稿"无面值和发行国名，图案过于精细，色彩繁杂，尺寸偏大，无法用作印制邮票的蓝本，同时推测画稿出自洋人之手，图案截自欧洲代印的中国钞票[2]。但这种说法没有任何依据，仅是推测而已。根据此次发现的德纳罗档案，可以认为，金登干 5 月 22 日信函中所提到的两份画稿极有可能是赫德遗集中的"双龙戏珠"和"龙凤戏珠"。这种设想基于以下三个重要理由：

1　参见本书附录"大龙邮品集萃"。
2　Philip W. Ireland, *CHINA —— The Large Dragons 1878 —1885,* p.16, 1978, Robson Lowe Ltd., London.

1."海关印记"——太极阴阳图案

在邮票的设计及纸张水印中采用太极阴阳图案，与赫德的主张相关。早在 1874 年 4 月 4 日，赫德致函金登干："采用阴阳图案做我们的'海关印记'[1] 好了。就像你画的那样，分别加上一个黑的或白的圆点。"[2] 我们在德纳罗档案中还可以看到一份《中国海关总税务司署伦敦办事处刷唛方法》，在这份文件中有两张示意图，均带有赫德要求的"海关印记"——太极阴阳图案。而且特别说明："大清海关印记的构图是一个圆绕着两个相等的半圆，即：右侧图形是黑色的，上半圆的中心或圆眼为白色，而左侧的半圆是白色的，圆眼为黑色。"因此，太极阴阳图案作为一个特殊标记，广泛应用在中国海关伦敦办事处的各项事务之中。

在 6 月 8 日的报告中，德纳罗公司特别说明，因为无法在纸张上取得满意的效果，故而在设计时去除了阴阳符号的圆眼。

然而，赫德所推崇的太极阴阳图并没有融入上海印制的大龙邮票，即德璀琳所主持设计的图案之中，也没有采用阴阳水印纸张印制，似乎没有得到赫德的"真传"。不过，后来小龙和万寿邮票部分面值的印制采用阴阳水印纸，似乎又在考虑"补救"。

---

1 《中国海关密档——赫德、金登干函电汇编（1874—1907）》将其翻译为"财产标记"，本文将其译为"海关印记"。
2 陈霞飞主编：《中国海关密档——赫德、金登干函电汇编（1874—1907）》（第一卷），北京：中华书局 1990 年版，第 23 页。译文有修改。

2."赫德画稿"与德纳罗设计稿的内在关联

"赫德画稿"源自赫德遗集,一为"双龙戏珠",另一为"龙凤戏珠",基本的图案结构:以太极阴阳为中心,双龙或一龙一凤分列两侧。"赫德画稿"与德纳罗公司后来为中国海关设计的邮票及邮资信封邮资符的中心图案结构基本一致,因此,"德纳罗设计稿"与"赫德画稿"之间存在着某种关联,换句话说,"赫德画稿"就是金登干信中所提到的来自北京的两幅画稿。

3. 太极阴阳图的阴阳位置

仔细甄别"赫德画稿"与"德纳罗设计稿",会发现其中的太极阴阳图案中的阴阳位置不尽相同,"赫德画稿"阴面在左,向下;而"德纳罗设计稿"阴面在右,向上。如果说"德纳罗设计稿"源自"赫德画稿",太极阴阳图的阴阳位置为何会发生如此变化?审阅档案,谜团迎刃而解。在 5 月 22 日发给德纳罗公司的信函中,金登干特别强调:"'阴阳'图案中,阴面应该朝上。"同时为了更为直观准确,金登干还在信函中绘制了一个草图,用以说明阴阳的位置。这样的修改说明,不仅为德纳罗公司的设计图案提出了明确的要求,同时也为我们把"赫德画稿"与北京寄来的画稿关联在一起提供了若干的提示。

在费拉尔 1896 年的《清朝邮政邮票和明信片——呈海关总税务

司备忘录》中，多处绘制太极阴阳符号[1]，其位置与金登干的要求一致，可以确认为海关的标准图位。由此，以往邮学资料中对海关使用阴阳符号的上下、正反的表述有待修正。

丽如银行[2]的钱币照片与"龙"图

在德纳罗档案第二页[3]的上边粘贴有一张照片，下边粘贴了一幅黄色基调的"龙"图，这两份资料是除两张画稿之外德纳罗公司设计邮票的重要参考资料。

首先我们先谈谈上边的这张照片，照片的上侧和右侧写有："Duplicate of a photo, lent me by Mr. Campbell, he having borrowed it from the Oriental Bank."（坎贝尔先生借给我的照片翻拍件，系其从丽如银行所借。）照片上共计五种钱币，其中标称"五分"、"一钱[4]"、"二钱"和"五钱"四种面值的钱币有正反面图案，另一枚最大的钱币没有带面值的正面图案，只有反面的八卦和太极阴阳图案，

1　参见《费拉尔手稿——清代邮政邮票和明信片备忘录》（人民邮电出版社1991年版）中的原件影印本。

2　第一家进入中国的外国银行，其前身为 1842 年由英国和印度合资的"西印度银行"（Bank of Western India），总行原设在印度孟买，1845 年迁至伦敦，更名为 Oriental Bank，后在香港、福州和上海等地设立分行，但名称不统一，在香港称为金宝银行，在福州称为东藩汇兑银行，在上海称为丽如银行。

3　参见本书德纳罗档案原本。

4　1 钱＝10 分。

图案下方注明"1 Tael"，即 1 两[1]。经仔细辨识，照片上非钱币实物，而是手绘设计图稿。查询钱币著作，图稿所示钱币就是泉界大名鼎鼎的关平两制银币"中外通宝"。

长期以来，"中外通宝"的身世之谜聚讼不已，有学者因为钱币中心的太极阴阳图案一度将其归入"朝鲜"钱币范畴，也有学者认为系属外国造币厂用于市场推广的商业币。耿爱德（E. Kann）提出是为了支付中国的海关税所试制，有可能在英国铸造，时间"（约）1858 年"[2]。1997 年，马传德和徐渊采信了 1987 年乔·克里达在《香港货币》中的论述，即"中外通宝"银币照片的最早发现时间是 1878 年，该币参照了"上海一两"银币设计方案，经香港造币厂厂长构思设计，由英国皇家造币厂铸制[3]。孙浩在《百年银圆》一书中指出，英国皇家造币厂博物馆所藏"中外通宝"全套 5 枚、币模及设计图均为香港造币厂前厂长乾打过世后，其家人于 1888 年所捐赠[4]。

此次发现的德纳罗档案，又为我们解读"中外通宝"的身世之谜提供了一个崭新的视角。首先，过去发现"中外通宝"银币照片的最早时间为 1878 年，而新发现的照片将时间又前推了一年；其次，

---

1 1 两＝10 钱＝100 分。

2 钱爱德著，钱屿、钱卫译：《中国币图说汇考 —— 金银镍铝》，北京：金城出版社 2014 年版，第 480-482 页。

3 马传德、徐渊：《揭开"中外通宝"银币之谜》，《中国钱币》1997 年第 4 期，第 45 页。

4 孙浩编著：《百年银圆》，上海：上海科学技术出版社 2016 年版，第 188-190 页。

档案中所存照片的提供方为丽如银行，可以确认"中外通宝"与丽如银行相关；第三，德纳罗公司在为中国海关设计邮票时把"中外通宝"作为参考，此套钱币一定与中国海关也有关联，这合理地解释了赫德所推崇的"海关印记"太极阴阳图案置于"中外通宝"中央的原因。

"中外通宝"设计稿照片为什么来自丽如银行？又为什么与中国海关密切相关？为了解答这些疑惑，还得从 1876 年的《滇案条约》[1]说起，该条约的签订起因于 1875 年"马嘉理事件"[2]，赫德参与了中英双方解决此事在烟台的谈判，并设想在条约中加上"铸银官局"和"送信官局"的相关内容，但最终未果。特别是"铸银官局"一事，不仅李鸿章不支持，英国驻华公使威妥玛也不表态，这让赫德愤愤不已。因为在此之前，他对造币厂问题谋划已久，曾数度为之咨询丽如银行，内容涉及造币厂的利润、工程估算、试制的样币、全年经营的费用和工厂的规划等问题[3]，时间从 1875 年 8 月至 1878 年 1 月。双方联系期间，丽如银行原来的经理斯图尔特病逝，彼得·坎

---

1 又称《中英会议条款》。英文本称为《英中两国政府全权大臣的协定》，通常简称为《烟台条约》。

2 1875 年，为了配合探查缅滇陆路的英国探路队，英国驻华公使派出翻译马嘉理南下迎接。双方在缅甸会合后，向云南边境进发。2 月 21 日，英国人在云南腾越与当地的少数民族发生冲突，马嘉理及数名随行人员被打死。史称"马嘉理事件"，或称"滇案"。

3 陈霞飞主编：《中国海关密档 —— 赫德、金登干函电汇编（1874—1907）》（第一卷），第 285、288-289、291、320-321、336、342、348、367、380、385、389、621 页；（第二卷），第 3 页，北京：中华书局 1990 年版。

贝尔继任其位，金登干曾向赫德汇报："我把造币厂的便函交给了已被任命为经理的坎贝尔。俟收到已故的斯图尔特存在巴伊亚那儿的文件后，他将于下星期料理此事。装有 5 枚硬币样品的盒子于本月 17 日寄给了上海和横滨该银行的代理人，随次一邮班又寄去了复制品。装有每种硬币 100 枚样品的盒子昨日已从南安普敦寄走，而复制品将于两周之后由同一线路发出。"[1]金登干在信中提及的"5 枚硬币样品"极有可能就是丽如银行提供给德纳罗公司那张照片上的 5 枚钱币，也就是上文提及的"中外通宝"，如果确实如此，那"中外通宝"铸制的时间也可以大致定为 1875 年底。此外，档案中照片的出借人"Mr. Campbell"，应该不是金登干（J.D. Campbell），而是丽如银行的继任经理彼得·坎贝尔（Peter Campbell）。

仔细观察"赫德画稿"、"中外通宝"和"德纳罗设计稿"，三者的主图均是双龙（一龙一凤）环抱阴阳，"赫德画稿"与"中外通宝"中间的太极阴阳图案均为"阴面朝下"，而"中外通宝"与"德纳罗设计稿"的图案几近一致，但"德纳罗设计稿"的太极阴阳图案根据金登干 5 月 22 日的信函要求改成了"阴面朝上"。图案的变化似乎反映了这样一种关系："赫德画稿"是"中外通宝"和"德纳罗设计稿"的母稿，"中外通宝"在前，"德纳罗设计稿"在后。

---

1 陈霞飞主编：《中国海关密档——赫德、金登干函电汇编（1874—1907）》（第一卷），北京：中华书局 1990 年版，第 336 页。

最后，我们再谈谈丽如银行钱币照片下边的"龙"图。"龙"图系金登干 5 月 22 日提供，从旗形、龙态以及龙珠的位置来看，是当时大清的三角官旗。1862 年，法国公使哥士耆向恭亲王奕訢提议中国水师增挂龙旗，曾国藩为之献策："拟用三角尖旗，大船直高一丈，小船旗高七八尺，其斜长及下横长各从其便，均用黄色画龙，龙头向上。"[1] 1874 年，应赫德要求，金登干在伦敦制作龙旗，以用作经总理各国事务衙门批准的海关船只标识旗[2]。此后，金登干就此事宜致函赫德，告知已寄运小旗样品，大旗样品因时间问题没有来得及发运，另有一种正在制作之中，并作简单的可行性分析[3]。德纳罗档案中金登干提供的图片基本可以认定为样旗制作过程中经过赫德认可的设计定稿。

1877 年中国海关与英国德纳罗公司之间的这段以筹印邮票为要旨的工作交往源自赫德开办邮政的设想，始于 1877 年 3 月 5 日德璀琳的询函。由此，德纳罗公司为中国海关撰写了详实的机密技术报告，专门设计了邮票、邮资信封和邮资符图稿，以及纸张水印图稿，但未被采用，双方的合作最终因赫德的指示而中断。英国德纳

---

1 宝鋆等修：《筹办夷务始末（同治朝）》（沈云龙主编"近代中国史料丛刊"第六十二辑）第二册卷九，台北：文海出版社 1971 年版，第 951-952 页。
2 陈霞飞主编：《中国海关密档——赫德、金登干函电汇编（1874—1907）》（第一卷），北京：中华书局 1990 年版，第 51-53 页。
3 同上，第 71-72 页。

罗公司在 1877 年中国海关为筹印邮票所作的探索活动中扮演了非常重要的角色，特别是所撰写的机密报告，为中国海关提供了极其宝贵的参考。英国德纳罗虽没能被中国海关遴选入围，但中国创设邮政的脚步并未就此搁浅，另择他路自行印制大龙邮票的帷幕也就此徐徐拉开。

赵　岳

2018 年 6 月

Foreword

Customs of China and De La Rue of England in 1877

As the first set of stamps issued by the Chinese Customs, the Large Dragon stamps draw great attention for their distinguished historical status. The background and dates of their issuance have been widely discussed among scholars. Moreover, due to the repeated printings of the Large Dragons, the plate settings that resulted are complex. Covers bearing the Large Dragons are scarce and are invaluable to Chinese philately, in addition to their long being objects of pleasure, appreciation and satisfaction to collectors of classic stamps.

In 1925, M.D. Chow presented an article in *Philatelic Bulletin*, which was an exploratory study on subjects such as the design, denominations, printed colors, issuance quantities and plate settings of the Large Dragons. In the 1940s, T.C. Chen, Sun Junyi, etc. successively published papers for carrying out further discussion on the Large Dragons in *Cathay Philatelic Journal*, *Chinese Philatelic Classics*, *New Light Philatelic Magazine* and *Philatelic Friends*. Sir Percival

David authored the paper *Sketches, Essays and Proofs of China's First Issue* in the March 1949 *The London Philatelist* (Volume 58, No. 676). His article introduced the Large Dragons' related drawings, design essays, as well as proofs and specimens for the master dies and clichés. To commemorate the 100th anniversary of the issuance of Large Dragon Stamps in 1978, Philip Willard Ireland released his renowned monograph, *CHINA ——The Large Dragons 1878 —1885*, which comprehensively and systematically covered the background and course of issuance, along with the clichés and plate settings of the stamps.

In 1980, Sun Zhiping's presentation *My Opinion on the Issuance Date of the Large Dragons* in *Philately* (Issue 3) sparked widespread and enthusiastic response from scholars. Quite a few Chinese philatelists and researchers on the Chinese Customs history published papers subsequently putting forth their opinions. This further opened up a large-scale nationwide philatelic discussion, focusing on the issuance date and background of the Large Dragons, which lasted for five long years. As a result, the consensus that emerged gradually cleared up the confusion surrounding the issuance date of the Large Dragons. The proposition of the stamps being issued in July of 1878 was subsequently confirmed with the aid of credible primary sources, which was the most important contribution from the Chinese philatelic community after the founding of the People's Republic.

Both the *Selected Archives of Tientsin Customs Post in Late Qing Dynasty*, co-edited by the Tianjin Archives and China Philatelic Press in 1988, and *Archives of China's Imperial Maritime Customs: Confidential Correspondence between Robert Hart and James Duncan Campbell, 1874*

—1907, Volumes I - IV, jointly compiled by the Second Historical Archives of China and Institute of Modern History of the Chinese Academy of Social Sciences between 1990 and 1993, with Chen Xiafei and Han Rongfang as the chief editors, furnished philatelists with important first-hand historical records on the background of the issuance of the Large Dragons. James B. Whang of Taiwan's *Whang's Illustrated Collection of the Large Dragons, 1878 —1885* and *A Comprehensive Illustration on Covers of Chinese Large Dragons* were published in 1993 and 1997, respectively, and have been the important references for collecting and researching the Large Dragons.

Since the 1878 release of the Large Dragon issue, many philatelists, at home and abroad, have been devoting lifelong efforts to studying and collecting the issue. Among the more prominent representative figures are John A. Agnew, Sir Percival David, Major James Starr, Dr. Warren G. Kauder, G. Gilbert, Philip W. Ireland, Paul P. Hock, Meiso Mizuhara, Anna-Lisa and Sven-Eric Beckeman, Jane and Dan Sten Olsson, M.D. Chow, Allen Gokson, C. Chen, James Huangco, James B. Whang, L.Y. Woo, Lam Man Yin, Lee King Yue, etc. G. Gilbert, Robert C.H. Lee, C. Chen, Paul P. Hock and the Beckemans in turn worked to identify the characteristic features for each plate setting based on existing material.

Tremendous research has been carried out on the Large Dragon issue for the past one hundred years, leading to numerous publications. The results were fruitful, and some of them were simply brilliant. Nonetheless, there are still a few mysteries waiting to be solved, especially those concerning the preparation and production of the issue during the period between 1876 and 1878. Due to

53

the lack of related documents, there still exist some missing links, academically speaking, and cognitive ambiguities. In fact, no really significant records had been unearthed for the past two decades, so that the academic community has been unable to make substantial research breakthroughs on the Large Dragons.

I took a special trip to London in late October 2017 in connection with my essay in Commemoration of the 140th Anniversary of the Issuance of the Large Dragon Stamps, part of the celebration program for the issue held this year co-hosted by the China National Postage Stamp Museum and China Customs Museum. I went through places like the British Library, the National Postal Museum, the University of Reading Library and the Museum of Philatelic History at the Royal Philatelic Society London, searching for evidence and records in piles and piles of literature that might be related in the slightest degree to the stamp production by the Chinese Imperial Customs 140 years ago. After almost relentless efforts, I was able to discover quite a number of important documents, including the Thomas De La Rue & Co.'s China Archives of 1877, which ultimately led to the publication of this book.

Beginning of the Relationship between the Chinese Customs and England's De La Rue in 1877

To emulate in China the operation of Western postal services, Robert Hart, the Inspector General of Chinese Imperial Maritime Customs, requested the Inspectors from all Customs Offices for their opinions on the topic in order to draw on their collective wisdom. It is surmised that this took place no later than the end of 1876[1], as suggested in *The History of Chinese Postage Stamps*. Among the existing documents available, the earliest one focusing on postage stamp production of the Imperial Customs was found to be a March 5, 1877 letter from Gustav Detring to James Duncan Campbell.[2] This record, preserved in the Tianjin Archives, presents Detring, the then-Inspector of the Chefoo Customs[3], inquiring of Campbell, the then-Commissioner of the London Office of the Inspectorate General of Chinese Imperial Maritime Customs, about the Inspector General's objectives. The questions raised by Detring were the following[4]:

　　1. What would say one million postage stamps made in England cost?

　　2. What would it cost to procure machinery, plant and paper to make it in China say one million stamps per week?

　　3. What would be the cost per month of the English

1　Editorial Committee of The History of Chinese Postage Stamps of Ministry of Information Industry of People's Republic of China ed., *The History of Chinese Postage Stamps*, Vol. I, p.101, 1999, The Commercial Press, Beijing.

2　Tianjin Archives and China Philatelic Publishing House ed., Xu Heping and Zhang Junhuan trans., *Selected Archives of Tientsin Customs Post in Late Qing Dynasty*, pp.23-25, 1988, China Philatelic Publishing House, Beijing.

3　Detring was assigned to be the Inspector of Tientsin Customs by the end of 1877.

4　Tianjin Archives and China Philatelic Publishing House ed., Xu Heping and Zhang Junhuan trans., *Selected Archives of Tientsin Customs Post in Late Qing Dynasty*, pp.23-25, 1988, China Philatelic Publishing House, Beijing.

personnel required for producing one million stamps a week, taking into consideration that all elementary manual labour can be had here.

Furthermore, Detring earnestly requested Campbell to respond quickly and additionally help finding "the latest and best compilation of English and French Postal Laws and the Postal blank forms in use"[1] of those two countries. Thereafter Campbell, on behalf of the Chinese Customs, officially made a succession of inquiries in London for the preparation of postage stamp production. Hence, the year of 1877 became an exceptionally special point in time in the history of Chinese postage stamps. To fulfill Detring's request, Campbell contacted Thomas De La Rue & Co. of London, which was a printing house with a long history, as well as strong technical expertise. This was the same "De La Rue" mentioned repeatedly in Campbell's letters and telegrams to Hart. There have been only a few references in the historical records available over the last the 140 years about the contacts between Campbell and De La Rue, none of which were directly related to this subject. This also made the Chinese Customs' early days of preparations for postage stamp production to be surrounded by some mystery. We noticed Detring's letter of inquiry, consisting of the three questions mentioned previously, was pasted on the first page of De La Rue's China Archives of

---

1 Tianjin Archives and China Philatelic Publishing House ed., Xu Heping and Zhang Junhuan trans., *Selected Archives of Tientsin Customs Post in Late Qing Dynasty*, p.24, 1988, China Philatelic Publishing House, Beijing

1877, and Campbell's name card was affixed to the lower left corner of the letter. The date of May 1, 1877 was indicated at the upper right. In fact, comparing it to the copy of Detring's letter in the Tianjin Archives, the English wording used for composing the three questions was exactly the same, except for the date. The inquiry letter in De La Rue's Archives was not signed. Based on handwriting analysis, the letter was written by neither Detring nor Campbell, and thus was copied by a third person. Each question was followed by an answer written in pencil, as follows:

1. *£50 to £60*
2. *Hypothetically*
3. *Will write full report*

De La Rue would have considered the inquiry "to procure machinery, plant and paper to make it in China" in the second question above bizarre and could not honor it. This obdurate decision of De La Rue not only resulted from its commercial interest but also from its biased opinion of then-Chinese technological ability. Subsequently, Campbell dutifully conveyed the message in his May 5 telegram No. 161 to Hart: "For Detring First postage Query fifty to sixty Pounds Second third considered impracticable Details ready in fortnight."[1]

1　Chen Xiafei and Han Rongfang chief ed., *Archives of China's Imperial Maritime Customs: Confidential Correspondence between Robert Hart and James Duncan Campbell, 1874—1907*, Vol. III, p.1057, 1992, Foreign Languages Press, Beijing.

Detring's letter of inquiry to Campbell, unchanged, was presented as the first page in De La Rue's China Archives of 1877. This is enough to illustrate the interaction between the two parties, originating from Hart's vision of creating the Chinese Imperial Post. De La Rue's Archives, therefore, become the concrete evidence for their related collaborations.

Collaboration Process between the Chinese Customs and England's De La Rue in 1877

Focusing on the three questions in the May 1, 1877 letter of inquiry, as relayed by Campbell, De La Rue began the process for implementing stamp designs and printing arrangements for stamp production. A few clues concerning the progress of this process can be found in the *Archives of China's Imperial Maritime Customs: Confidential Correspondence between Robert Hart and James Duncan Campbell, 1874—1907*. In the following paragraphs, we will rearrange its relevant contents, along with our latest findings, in a chronological manner to facilitate a better interpretation of this part of the history.

May 5 was the fourth day after Campbell had made his first official contact with De La Rue. He provided Detring with the preliminary answers in his telegram to Hart. Instead of forwarding the message directly to Detring, he relayed it through Hart. This was an explicit indication that Campbell did not want to bypass his superior, Hart, about the matter. By means of this small gesture, he simultaneously hinted all subsequent activities would proceed smoothly only by gaining Hart's support and approval. By May 11,

Campbell submitted another report to Hart and mentioned the document, as requested by Detring, would only be completed in the coming week. He particularly commented that Henry C.J. Kopsch, the then-Inspector of Kiukiang Customs, also wanted information for a "postage system" he was "trying to get up."[1]

On both May 22 and 23, Campbell sent a letter to De La Rue. These letters were meant to assist De La Rue with the stamp designs. Additionally, Campbell attached the "two sketches I received from Peking" and "a sketch of the Dragon", according to his first letter, to be used as references. In his letter of May 23, Campbell made an explanation on the symbol of "Yin & Yang" as it appeared in the sketches furnished on the 22nd.

De La Rue submitted a 42-page confidential report by June 8. The original date of this report, June 8, was crossed out in pencil and with a note at the left "Mr. Campbell altered this date to the 18th, see his letter of June 29, 1877." De La Rue was asked to change the date of its report, and this might be due to Campbell's not accomplishing his portion of the work within the time originally planned. Campbell in his June 22 letter to Hart mentioned Detring's request again, stating "I am writing you an official on the subject of the reference made to me by Detring on postal matters, more than two months ago, and I hope that the information will be useful."[2]

1　Chen Xiafei and Han Rongfang chief ed., *Archives of China's Imperial Maritime Customs: Confidential Correspondence between Robert Hart and James Duncan Campbell, 1874 —1907*, Vol. I, p.272, 1990, Foreign Languages Press, Beijing.

2　Ibid., p.283.

The "official" mentioned in this letter should be related to De La Rue's June 8 report.

On July 5 and 6, De La Rue and Campbell each sent two letters to the other party. The contents were mainly centered on requisitions soliciting tenders presented by Campbell. There were a total of six different requisitions, without indication of a due date, consisting of to-be-purchased items, comprising surface-printing machines, perforating machines, printing inks, paper, gum and letter scales, respectively. This might have been the wishful thinking on the part of Campbell that De La Rue would fully cooperate in fulfilling these orders, if the Inspectorate General decided to produce its stamps in China. On the other hand, De La Rue repeatedly emphasized the items listed in the orders were unable alone to fulfill the requirements for printing stamps. At the same time, De La Rue clearly stated, from the anti-counterfeiting point of view, its Company would be the best possible choice for manufacturing the stamps needed by the Chinese Customs.

Analyzing the contents of these letters, De La Rue should have received the requisitions by July 2. On July 4 or two days later, both parties had a meeting on the implementation of these orders, but De La Rue was reluctant to tender. After this unpleasant meeting, Campbell telegraphed Hart: "Postal requisition impracticable Machine Paper Ink all unsuitable Elaborate report mailed twenty second June If you send immediately design for last stamp British postage size and telegraph instructions upon receipt report all kinds can be delivered here ten weeks afterwards price fifty five Pound per Million Special experience required Time expense saved & protection from forgery ensured by starting manufacture here transferring to China afterwards."[1] Moreover, the telegram was copied and sent to De La Rue on July 5. Comparing the English texts in these two copies of the telegram, the contents were basically the same, except for two small differences. In the telegram sent to Hart, the cost per million for producing stamps was quoted at £55, and, on the other hand, it was written as £54 in the copy for De La Rue. If this interesting phenomenon was not caused by a slip of the pen, the underlying reason is indeed worth thinking about deeply. For those who may be interested, please refer to *Archives of China's Imperial Maritime Customs: Confidential Correspondence between Robert Hart and James Duncan Campbell , 1874 —1907*, Volume I, p.320. The letter No. A/144 in the section, focusing on commissions, may provide some hints. The other discrepancy was the line "design for last stamp British postage size" mentioned in the telegram to Hart, with the wording changed instead to "design for each stamp" in De La Rue's copy. No documents have been found related to the so-called "design for last stamp British postage size." However, one thing is certain that Campbell did not want De La Rue to have knowledge on this particular matter.

In his July 6 letter to Hart regarding the previously mentioned requisitions, Campbell wrote: "I have been put in a fix by Detring's Requisition for postage stamps. ——Even if I were to order the

---

1 Chen Xiafei and Han Rongfang chief ed., *Archives of China's Imperial Maritime Customs: Confidential Correspondence between Robert Hart and James Duncan Campbell, 1874 —1907*, Vol. III, pp.1058-1059, 1992, Foreign Languages Press, Beijing.

things, they would be ready for 3 or 4 months. Shall not be able to send Detring as I wished copy of my dispatch which I have to write very hurriedly."[1] On July 13, Campbell addressed another letter to Hart, concerning the requisitions again: "I have but little to add to my despatches, in re Postage Stamps. The delay will, no doubt, cause your disappointment, ——but even if I had ordered the things from the firms named in the Requisitions, six months would probably elapse before they all reached Shanghai——leaving a margin for contractors' delays, accidents, etc. etc. etc. By employing De La Rue's, not only will the order be properly executed, but time and expense will be saved. If you decide upon the manufacture being commenced here, it may be well perhaps to send the perforating machine to China, so that the stamps could not be issued until they had undergone this last process, ——and check——in China."[2]

The above two letters clearly indicate that the six requisitions included in De La Rue's Archives were made at Detring's request. In fact, Detring had remitted £1,000 to the London Office of the Inspectorate General of the Imperial Maritime Customs in May to purchase the items[3]. According to the July 4 telegram, De La Rue, in terms of specific implementation time, would take about 10 weeks,

---

1 Chen Xiafei and Han Rongfang chief ed., *Archives of China's Imperial Maritime Customs: Confidential Correspondence between Robert Hart and James Duncan Campbell, 1874-1907*, Vol. I, p.286, 1990, Foreign Languages Press, Beijing.

2 Ibid., pp.286-287.

3 Tianjin Archives and China Philatelic Publishing House ed., Xu Heping and Zhang Junhuan trans., *Selected Archives of Tientsin Customs Post in Late Qing Dynasty*, p.165, 1988, China Philatelic Publishing House, Beijing.

or two and half months, to complete the stamp production. If these stamps were manufactured in China, the time required for acquiring related materials and equipment would be three to four months, according to Campbell's July 6 letter. Nonetheless, Campbell did not make any suggestions on which to select between the two. However, in Campbell's July 13 letter, he was straightforward enough to state that employment of De La Rue for stamp production might save manpower. He also emphasized the possible delay caused by other suppliers, and the items would take a possible period of six months before reaching Shanghai. Although Campbell seemed to make a regular progress report, his inclination was obvious. Surely, Hart would also be fully aware of the situation.

On July 20, Campbell wrote in his letter to Hart, "Receiving your Z/6 of 2 June, but your Z/5 must have gone down in the *Meikong*, also with, I fear, Detring's explanatory Memo. on postal matters."[1] In fact, Campbell had already informed De La Rue of the shipwreck on July 5.

Hart, on October 25, wrote to Campbell and stated as follows, "Many thanks for De La Rue's long report. We'll get our[2] stamps made there, but I don't want to follow the sanguine Detring too rashly. I must feel my footing to be secure before attempting to

---

1 Chen Xiafei and Han Rongfang chief ed., *Archives of China's Imperial Maritime Customs: Confidential Correspondence between Robert Hart and James Duncan Campbell, 1874—1907*, Vol. I, p.289, 1990, Foreign Languages Press, Beijing.

2 The word "out" was printed in the original text. We feel "out" is inappropriately used in this content and should be a typo. Hence, it is changed to the word "our".

push on."[1] The "long report", as stressed by Hart, should be De La Rue's June 8 confidential letter. Although Hart expressed the stamps would be manufactured by De La Rue, he did not give Campbell any clear instructions on the next step in the following two months or so.

In mid-December 1877, the London Office of the Chinese Imperial Maritime Customs finally had its first collaboration, in a real sense, with De La Rue, for the order of "1,000 dark green cloth boards", which would be the exquisite covers for housing the hardback French version of *Le Saint Edit*, translated by A.T. Piry. Based on information gathered from the Archives, the order was delayed until 1878, and the other details have yet to be discovered. The copies of *Le Saint Edit*, published in 1879 and kept in libraries, such as the National Library of China, British Library, etc., were the results of this Sino-British collaboration. Was it Campbell's idea of interspersing this requisition order, as a matter of expediency, to maintain the status quo with De La Rue while waiting for Hart's further instructions? Was it eventually related to the failure of the postage stamp production venture? The answers are difficult to discern.

Not having received any explicit instructions from Hart, Campbell telegraphed Hart on January 4, 1878, urging him to take action: "Detring has sent order postage stamps Shall I

---

1 Chen Xiafei and Han Rongfang chief ed., *Archives of China's Imperial Maritime Customs: Confidential Correspondence between Robert Hart and James Duncan Campbell, 1874 —1907*, Vol. I, p.314, 1990, Foreign Languages Press, Beijing.

proceed with order."[1] After sending the telegram to Hart, Campbell forwarded a letter to Hart on the same day, numbered A/147, writing: "Mr. De La Rue has frequently enquired if I had heard from you in reference to his memo. I have conveyed to him your thanks for the same."[2] Later in the day, Campbell wrote another letter, numbered A/148, to Hart, reporting Detring's reactions on De La Rue's report, and Detring had written concerning the postage stamps: "now send you enclosed four designs which have been adopted by the Inspector General for the various Haikuan[3] values required. The designs are of course to be reduced to ordinary postage stamp dimensions. The colours to be used are, you will observe, sufficiently explained in the enclosure."[4] Detring's letter was accompanied by four sketches of the stamp designs. From late December 1877, when Hart received De La Rue's report, to early January 1878, when Campbell telegraphed to urge him to authorize the postage stamp production in London, Hart did not specifically express his position on when production should be initiated. Although Campbell had always been reporting about Detring's latest sentiments in his letters, his feelings of anxiety and impatience were also well reflected reading between the lines. To avoid any possible

---

1　Chen Xiafei and Han Rongfang chief ed., *Archives of China's Imperial Maritime Customs: Confidential Correspondence between Robert Hart and James Duncan Campbell, 1874 —1907*, Vol. III, p.1066, 1992, Foreign Languages Press, Beijing.

2　Ibid., Vol. I, p.333, 1990.

3　"Haikuan" is the Chinese way of saying "Customs".

4　Chen Xiafei and Han Rongfang chief ed., *Archives of China's Imperial Maritime Customs: Confidential Correspondence between Robert Hart and James Duncan Campbell, 1874 —1907*, Vol. I, p.334, 1990, Foreign Languages Press, Beijing.

misunderstanding from Hart and at the same time prove his loyalty, Campbell added, before ending the letter: "The Enclosure is an 'order for Postage Stamps to be transmitted through the Non-Resident Secretary London' —and after the observation made in your A/46 —that you must feel your footing to be sure before attempting to push on and shall not give the order for the quantities required, until receipt of your instructions." [1]

On February 24, Hart replied to Campbell's January 4 telegram and announced: "Defer Postage stamp order."[2] This message from Hart basically put a complete stop to the preparatory work for postage stamp production in London, as well as to the potential collaboration between the Chinese Customs and England's De La Rue.

As recorded in the literature, the four sketched stamp designs sent from China by Detring were actually submitted and approved in May 1877. They were then forwarded to Campbell in November.[3] The designs were those of "Dragon Couchant", "Phoenix", "Elephant with Wang Nian Ching Flowers" and "Pagoda",[4] respectively. Based on the described design contents, the essays of the following three designs, the "Dragon Couchant", "Elephant with Wang

---

1 Chen Xiafei and Han Rongfang chief ed., *Archives of China's Imperial Maritime Customs: Confidential Correspondence between Robert Hart and James Duncan Campbell, 1874 —1907*, Vol. I, p.334, 1990, Foreign Languages press, Beijing.

2 Ibid., Vol. III, p.1069, 1992.

3 Tianjin Archives and China Philatelic Publishing House ed., Xu Heping and Zhang Junhuan trans., *Selected Archives of Tientsin Customs Post in Late Qing Dynasty*, pp.164-165, 1988, China Philatelic Publishing House, Beijing.

4 Du Shengyu, *Sketches and Essays of the Large Dragons, Philately*, No.10, p.20, 1988.

Nian Ching Flowers" and "Pagoda", should be the ones from the Mizuhara collection. The "Dragon Couchant" was the design finally approved for the Large Dragon Issue. The word "couchant" was used as an expression to describe the coiled shape of a dragon, with its body resting on the four legs and its head raised above the shoulders. After receiving the detailed report and stamp designs submitted by De La Rue, why did Detring reciprocally furnish De La Rue with the Customs' own designs? Why did Hart unexpectedly terminate the collaborative process with De La Rue? Further studies may be needed to search for the reasons behind these actions.

Design Sketches of De La Rue for the Chinese Customs in 1877

De La Rue's June 8, 1877 long report touched on the essential elements of its printing technology. Hence, the word "confidential" was added to the top of the first page of the report. Taking into consideration the then-national conditions of China, along with the adaptabilities, as well as the pros and cons of the printing processes, the report explained exhaustively the technical details of the printing systems and also made some specific recommendations to the Chinese Customs. The original text covered a total 42 pages. To allow the policy makers, situated far away in China, to understand visually the end results of each process, De La Rue supplemented the report with 12 Appendices, from Appendix A to L, as detailed in the following table.

Appendix	Contents of Appendix
A	Specimens of stamps produced by four different printing processes
B	Different responses of stamps respectively printed using fugitive and ordinary inks after being treated with benzine
C	Photograph of an obliterating machine and specimen of the obliteration
D	Photograph of an obliterator installed with a pair of stamps and the sketch of an obliteration showing name of cancelling station and date
E	Specimens printed, respectively, using three different types of "doubly fugitive" inks
F	Pieces of ungummed watermarked stamp paper and gummed stamp paper
G	Specimen of a postage envelope for English Government
H	Specimens of the two kinds or duties of postage envelopes for India
I	Design sketches of postage envelope and embossed stamps of two denominations for Chinese Customs
J	Design sketches of watermark and two postage stamps for Chinese Customs
K	Specimen of quarter sheet of Hong Kong 12 cents
L	Specimen of "Stamped Paper" of India

Unfortunately, the above original Appendices were not included in De La Rue's 1877 Archives, except for a photograph of Appendix I.

Appendix J was exhibited publicly in the 100th Anniversary of Postage Stamp Printing of De La Rue & Co. exhibition held in 1955. Two sets of transparencies, containing pictures of the exhibits, were kept by the Postal Museum and Spink of London, respectively. These descriptions were written at the top of the exhibit page: "In 1877 we were approached by Mr. James D. Campbell, Commissioner of Customs, China, From the London Office of the Inspectorate General of Chinese Imperial Maritime Customs, to submit a proposal for printing stamps. Appendix J was submitted on June 18, 1877." *The DE LA RUE HISTORY of BRITISH & FOREIGN POSTAGE STAMPS, 1855 to 1901,* published by the Royal Philatelic Society London in 1958, recorded the stamp design sketches of Appendix J[1], and *The De La Rue Collection*, published by the Royal Philatelic Society London in 2014, also included the exhibit page containing Appendix J.[2]

Appendix A was also exhibited, along with Appendix J, in 1955, and is likewise shown in *The De La Rue Collection*.[3] However, De La Rue purposely affixed a set of the Large Dragons to the lower part of the exhibit page including Appendix A in the 1955 Exhibition. This might reflect the exploratory efforts contributed by De La Rue in 1877 to the Imperial Customs' preparation for its own stamp production.

Appendices I and J consisted of the following items:

1. specimens of the postage envelope designed,
2. two design sketches of the postage emblems, in circular and

---

1　*John Easton, The DE LA RUE HISTORY of BRITISH & FOREIGN POSTAGE STAMPS, 1855 to 1901, plate48, 1958, Faber and Faber, London.*

2　Frank Walton, *The De La Rue Collection*, p.2567, 2014, The Royal Philatelic Society, London.

3　Ibid., p.2566.

ellipsoidal forms, respectively, for the postage envelopes,

3. sketch for the watermark symbol of Yin & Yang, and

4. six stamp design sketches, three of each, in vertical and horizontal formats, respectively.

In Appendix I, written above the specimens for the postage envelope design is "Specimens of the proposed Postage Envelope for China, one showing the front, the other the back." On top of the design sketches for the postage designs is the notation "Sketches of the proposed stamps to be embossed on the above envelopes." In Appendix J, the description at the top of the exhibit page including the symbol of Yin & Yang is "Sketch of the watermark to be made in the paper employed for the Postage Stamps for China." The title for the specimens of the stamp designs is "Alternative sketches of the proposed Postage Stamps for China, the duties are merely suppositions." Two additional proofs were attached to the bottom of Appendix J and entitled "Engraver's proofs of adhesive stamps with an animal or a bird in the centre."

Appendix I consisted of two types of sketches for the postage designs. The denomination of the circular design in red was 1 Cent, and the denomination of the ellipsoidal one in green was 2 Cents. The alternative design sketches for postage stamps were categorized in two groups which were in horizontal and vertical formats, respectively. Each group consisted of three denominations, namely 1 Cent, 2 Cents and 5 Cents. The 1 Cent, 2 Cents and 5 Cents, in each format, were printed in red, green and yellow, respectively. These colors were chosen because the five different colors and their

associated representations were written in pencil on the bottom half
of the first page of the De La Rue's China Achieves as follows:

Yellow   Imperial colour

Red & Pink   Happy

Blue   Mourning

Green   Happy

Brown   Mourning

The colors of yellow, red and green had been selected by De
La Rue for its stamp designs, with yellow, representing the imperial
color, adopted for the highest denomination of 5 Cents. The same
three colors were ultimately employed for producing the Large
Dragons. The 1 Candarin, 3 Candarins and 5 Candarins of the
Large Dragons were printed in green, red and yellow, respectively.
Was this simply a coincidence or related to the suggestions of De La
Rue? No conclusion has been reached to date.

Relationship between
Hart Sketches and De La Rue Design Sketches

Campbell sent the two small sketches received from Peking to
De La Rue on May 22, 1877, with a postscript "Will you kindly
return the two small sketches, when you have done with them." In
his May 23 letter he pointed out: "In each of the two small sketches
I sent you yesterday, there is a globe, floating in space, which is
intended for the Yin & Yang." Thus, we may conclude there were

two small size sketches sent from Peking, and each sketch bore a symbol of Yin & Yang at the center. As Campbell specifically requested their return, De La Rue was unable to retain the sketches in its Archives. What exactly was shown in these sketches? The notion of two sketches, however, reminds us of the sketches of "Two Dragons Playing with a Pearl" and "Dragon and Phoenix Playing with a Pearl"[1] from Hart's personal collection, which will be referred to as the "Hart Sketches". Without corroboration from actual documents, there had been divergent opinions on the actual use of the Hart Sketches for a long while. A few scholars had noted the Hart Sketches were designed without value and issuing country. The designs were also too detailed, the colors too numerous and the overall size too great to form the basic blueprints for postage stamp printing. The same group also suggested the Hart Sketches were drawn by a Western artist as the central designs for Chinese banknotes to be printed in Europe.[2] However, there was no under-lying documentary evidence for this argument, and it was treated merely as a speculation. Based on our discoveries in the De La Rue's China Archives, with Campbell's May 22 letter as a clue, the two sketches he mentioned should very well be the sketches of "Two Dragons Playing with a Pearl" and "Dragon and Phoenix Playing with a Pearl" from Hart's personal collection. This proposition is based on the following three important reasons:

---

1 Refer to the collection of the Large Dragons in the Appendix of this book.
2 Philip W. Ireland, *CHINA——The Large Dragons 1878—1885*, p.16, 1978, Robson Lowe Ltd., London.

1. The Broad Arrow: Yin & Yang Device

The employment of the symbol of Yin & Yang Device in postage stamp designs, as well as in paper watermarks, was related to the consistent position of Hart. As early as April 4, 1874, Hart wrote to Campbell "Adopt the Yin & Yang device, as our 'broad arrow.' It is as you draw it with a black and a white eye added."[1] Additionally, there was a copy of the *London Office Inspectorate General of Chinese Maritime Customs: DIRECTIONS FOR MARKING CASES, &c.* in the De La Rue's China Archives. This document included two illustrations, both of which bore the "Broad Arrow", as requested by Hart. Furthermore, the "Broad Arrow" was the symbol of "Yin & Yang Device" described thus: "The Mark is constructed describing by two equal semi-circles with a circle round them, thus: the right side of the figure is dark, having the centre or eye of the upper semi-circle bright, whilst the left side is bright and the eye dark." In fact, the Yin & Yang Device, as a special sign representing the Chinese Imperial Maritime Customs, had been widely used in various customs affairs at the London Office of the Inspectorate General of Chinese Customs.

In its June 8 report, De La Rue also submitted "a design for what we should consider would be an appropriate watermark to employ in the paper for Chinese stamps. This consists of the symbol of Yin & Yang, deprived, however, of the nuclei, as those we could

---

1　Chen Xiafei and Han Rongfang chief ed., *Archives of China's Imperial Maritime Customs: Confidential Correspondence between Robert Hart and James Duncan Campbell, 1874 —1907*, Vol. I, p.9, 1990, Foreign Languages Press, Beijing.

not render satisfactorily in the paper."

However, this highly praised symbol of Yin & Yang Device by Hart was not assimilated into the subsequent production of the Large Dragons in Shanghai. The stamp design, presided over by Detring, was not the only element without the complement of Yin & Yang Device. The paper was made without the symbol as well. In short, Detring expunged Hart's "flavor" from China's first set of stamps. Nevertheless, the employment of Yin & Yang watermarked paper in the production of the later Dowager and Small Dragon Issues seemed a remedy for this exclusion.

2. The Intrinsic Relationship between the Hart Sketches and De La Rue Design Sketches

The Hart Sketches came from Hart's personal collection. One sketch was "Two Dragons Playing with a Pearl", and the other "Dragon and Phoenix Playing with a Pearl." The basic composition of the sketches adopted the symbol of Yin & Yang at their center and one dragon, or one dragon and one phoenix, positioned at each side. The thematic subjects for the central designs of both the Hart Sketches and De La Rue Sketches, which were later submitted to the Chinese Customs as De La Rue's proposed postage stamps and postage envelope emblems, were fundamentally similar. Accordingly, there is a distinct correlation between the Hart Sketches and De La Rue Design Sketches. In other words, the Hart Sketches should be the two sketches from Peking mentioned in Campbell's May 22 and 23 letters to De La Rue.

3. The Positions of Yin & Yang

After examining closely the Hart Sketches and De La Rue Design Sketches, we found the positions of Yin & Yang, in their respective Yin & Yang Devices, were not exactly the same. In the Hart Sketches, the Yins, or dark sides, were on the left and facing downward. Conversely, the Yins in the De La Rue design sketches were on the right and facing upward. If the composition of De La Rue Design Sketches originated from the Hart Sketches, why did the positions of Yin & Yang in the Device change completely? The answer to this question is easily discerned after seeing the De La Rue China Archives. In Campbell's May 22 letter to De La Rue, he particularly emphasized "In the Yin & Yang device, the dark side should be uppermost." To be more explicit and accurate, Campbell drew a sketch in his letter to describe the proper positions of Yin & Yang. This explanation of the modification furnished to De La Rue in the explicit design requirement provides us with the key to connect the Hart Sketches and the two sketches from Peking together.

In R.A. de Villard's 1896 *Proposed Stamps, & Postcards, etc. for the Imperial Chinese Post, Memos submitted to the Inspector General of I.M. Customs*, quite a few symbols of the Yin & Yang were presented.[1] The positions of Yin & Yang were consistent with Campbell's requirement. This might thus be recognized as the standard logo for the

---

1 Refer to the archives' photocopy in *Proposed Stamps, etc. & Postcards for the Imperial Chinese Post Memos.*

Chinese Imperial Customs. Therefore, the presentations of these Yin & Yang Devices in the literature as to whether they were described in their upright, inverted, reversed or reversely inverted positions should be revised.

Photograph of Coins of Oriental Bank[1]
and Sketch of a Dragon

A photograph was attached to the upper half of the second page in the De La Rue's Archives, and a sketch of a dragon, with a yellow tone, was affixed right beneath. These two items were references as important as the two sketches from Peking for De La Rue's production of the postage stamp designs.

Along the top and right frames of the photograph is the annotation "Duplicate of a photo, lent me by Mr. Campbell, he having borrowed it from the Oriental Bank." Five different coins are shown in the photograph. Both the obverse and reverse are displayed for the "5 Cents", "1 Mace"[2], "2 Mace" and "5 Mace". For the largest coin, only the reverse, with the design of Pa-Kua and Yin & Yang but without the denomination, is shown, with

---

1 The Oriental Bank was the first foreign bank in China. Its predecessor was Bank of Western India, a joint venture of Great Britain and India in 1842. The headquarters was originally established in Mumbai. It was relocated to London in 1845 and renamed the Oriental Bank. Branches were set up in Hong Kong, Foochow and Shanghai, but their Chinese names were all different. The Bank went bankrupt in 1892.

2 1 Mace=10 Cents.

"1 Tael"[1] written underneath. Upon close examination, we found that the items in the picture were not real coins but rather hand-drawn design sketches. We went through numismatic literature and realized these were the well-known Zhongwai Tongbao silver coins, produced based on the Customs' standardized weight of one tael, of the numismatic world.

The Zhongwai Tongbao have seemed an unsolvable mystery for a long time. Some scholars once classified the silver coins as those of North Korea due to the symbol of Yin & Yang at the coin's center. On the other hand, some considered they were produced by a foreign mint to be promoted as commercial coins. E. Kann posited the coins might have been minted as a trial for coinage to pay Chinese Customs duty. They seemed to have been minted in England around 1858.[2] In 1997 Ma Chuande and Xu Yuan stated in a published paper[3], based on an article by Joe Cribb who was then the Keeper of Coins and Medals at the British Museum in *Hong Kong Currency*, that the earliest recorded discovery of a photograph exhibiting the Zhongwai Tongbao silver coins was in 1878 and that these coins were conceived and designed by the director of Hong Kong Mint using the design scheme for "Shanghai One Tael" and were later produced by the Royal Mint. In *Silver & Gold Coins of China 1838 —1949*, which he edited, Sun Hao pointed out that the Zhongwai

---

1 1 Tael=10 Mace=100 Cents.

2 E. Kann, Qian Yu and Qian Wei trans., *Illustrated Catalogue of Chinese Coins: Gold, Silver, Nickel and Aluminum*, pp.480-482, 2014, Gold Wall Press, Beijing.

3 Ma Chuande and Xu Yuan, *Unveiling the Mystery of Zhongwai Tongbao Silver Coins*, *China Numismatics*, No. 4, pp.43-47,1997.

Tongbao in the Royal Mint Museum were a set of five coins which were donated, along with their master dies and design sketches, by the family of Thomas William Kinder, one-time director of the Hong Kong Mint, in 1888 after his death.[1]

The present discovery of the De La Rue China Archives furnishes us with a brand-new perspective to interpret the mystery of the Zhongwai Tongbao. Firstly, the earliest photograph of the Zhongwai Tongbao had been previously 1878. Secondly, the photograph kept in the De La Rue Archives was mentioned to have been provided by the Oriental Bank. Hence, it is not too difficult to conclude that the Zhongwai Tongbao silver coins were related to the Oriental Bank. Lastly, De La Rue used these silver coins as important reference during the process of designing postage stamps for the Chinese Customs. Therefore, this set of coins should likewise be closely related to the Chinese Customs. This reasonably may explain the positioning of the Yin & Yang Device, so highly advocated by Hart, at the center of the Zhongwai Tongbao.

Let's now ask ourselves the following questions. Why did the photograph of the designs of the Zhongwai Tongbao come from the Oriental Bank? Why was the Zhongwai Tongbao closely related to the Imperial Customs of China? To resolve these outstanding questions, we must start with the Chefoo Convention of 1876.[2] The

---

1 Sun Hao ed., *Silver & Gold Coins of China 1838 — 1949*, pp.188-190, 2016, Shanghai Scientific and Technical Publishers, Shanghai.

2 The Chefoo Convention was also known as the Agreement between the Plenipotentiary Ministers of the British and Chinese Governments.

Convention was signed as a result of the 1875 Margary Affair.[1] Hart participated in the Sino-British settlement negotiations of the Margary Affair in Chefoo and envisaged the addition of a couple relevant items to the treaty, like Bureau of Silver Casting and Bureau of Letter Posting, but ultimately failed. Li Hongzhang in particular did not support the establishment of the Bureau of Silver Casting, and Thomas Wade, the then-British Ambassador to China, also withheld his support. This outcome made Hart indignant. Long before the Chefoo Convention, Hart had consulted with the Oriental Bank on several occasions concerning various subjects, such as the actual profit of running a mint, evaluations of mint projects, production of specimen coins, annual cost for running the establishment, new arrangements and improvements with a view to economize the operation, etc.[2] During the period of contact between the two parties, from August 1875 to January 1878, Stuart, the manager of the Oriental Bank, passed away, and Peter Campbell succeeded him. J.D. Campbell wrote to Hart and reported as "I handed the note anent Minting to Campbell who has been appointed Manager. He will attend to the matter next week, after

---

1　In 1875, a junior British diplomat, Augustus Raymond Margary, was sent from Shanghai to Bhamo in Upper Burma, where he was supposed to meet the British Expedition Force, in an effort to explore overland trade routes between British India and the Chinese Provinces. On February 21, the British confronted the native people in Tengyueh, Yunnan. Margary and his four Chinese staff were killed. This was the so-called "Margary Affair" or "Yunnan Case".

2　Chen Xiafei and Han Rongfang chief ed., *Archives of China's Imperial Maritime Customs: Confidential Correspondence between Robert Hart and James Duncan Campbell, 1874 —1907*, Vol. I, pp.146-334, 1990, Foreign Languages Press, Beijing.

the receipt of poor Stuart's papers from Bahia. Boxes containing five specimen coins were posted to the Bank's Agents at Shanghai & Yokohama on the 17th instant and duplicates were sent by the following Mail. Boxes containing one hundred specimens of each coin left Southampton yesterday, and duplicates will be forwarded by the same route a fortnight hence."[1] The five specimen coins mentioned in Campbell's letter were most likely the five Zhongwai Tongbao silver coins in the photograph lent to De La Rue. If this were in fact the case, the limited mintage of the Zhongwai Tongbao could have occurred at the end of 1875. Moreover, the Mr. Campbell who lent the photograph should not be J.D. Campbell but Peter Campbell, the new manager of the Oriental Bank.

The central designs for the Hart Sketches, the Zhongwai Tongbao and De La Rue Design Sketches consist of similar patterns, such as the "two dragons", or "one dragon and one phoenix", embracing the Yin & Yang Device which was positioned right at the center. The Yin & Yang Devices in both the Hart Sketches and the Zhongwai Tongbao had their dark sides facing downward. The designs for both the Zhongwai Tongbao and De La Rue Design Sketches were very similar. As a reminder, Campbell requested De La Rue to change the dark side to "uppermost" on May 22. In fact, the change of this particular detail seems to yield a special kind of subtle relationship, as the Hart Sketches were the master designs for the Zhongwai

---

1 Chen Xiafei and Han Rongfang chief ed., *Archives of China's Imperial Maritime Customs: Confidential Correspondence between Robert Hart and James Duncan Campbell, 1874 —1907*, Vol. I, p.172, 1990, Foreign Languages Press, Beijing.

Tongbao and De La Rue Design Sketches, and the Zhongwai Tong-bao was earlier than De La Rue Design Sketches.

Finally, let's not forget the sketch of a dragon, placed right under the photograph of the Zhongwai Tongbao. The sketch was provided by Campbell on May 22. According to the shape of the flag, the form of the dragon and the position of the pearl, this should be the triangular Qing then-official flag. In 1862, Michel Alexandre Kleczkowski, France's Ambassador to China, suggested to the Prince Gong, Yixin, that Chinese naval vessels should hang the Flag of the Dragon. Zeng Guofan then proposed the employment of triangular flags with pointed tips. For large ships, the flags should be as tall as three meters. For smaller vessels, the length of the flags should be between two and two and half meters. There would be no restrictions on the length of its slope and width of the lower transverse section. The dragon should be painted in yellow, and the dragon head should be pointing upward.[1] In 1874, Campbell had the Dragon Flags made in London at Hart's request, which would be used as the flags for Chinese Customs vessels, as approved by the Ministry of Foreign Affairs of the Tsungli Yamen.[2] Then, Campbell replied to Hart: "I have enquired about Flags and am only waiting for one which is being made as a pattern, to send you my report.

---

1 Bao Yun *et al.* ed., *The Whole Course of Make Preparations Foreign Affairs, Reign of Tongzhi*, Vol. 2, No. 9, Shen Yunlung chief ed., *Modern Chinese Historical Materials Series*, No. 62, pp.951-952, 1971, Wenhai Press Co., Taipei.

2 Chen Xiafei and Han Rongfang chief ed., *Archives of China's Imperial Maritime Customs: Confidential Correspondence between Robert Hart and James Duncan Campbell, 1874—1907*, Vol. I, p.22, 1990, Foreign Languages Press, Beijing.

You will effect a great saving by ordering them from England. Would it not also be much cheaper to indent on England for the cloth and serge etc., required for uniforms —and also for Paint for boats, etc.! Upon the last item I fancy the saving would be very considerable." Afterwards, Campbell wrote another letter to Hart on the matter, informing him the samples for the small flags had been shipped. The large flags had not been dispatched due to some delays. The other kind was still being made. Campbell also conducted a simple feasibility study: "Printing is not practicable for the larger sizes of flags, and for the smaller sizes the first expense of the blocks would be very great, whilst the cost of their manufacture would be little less than that of painted flags. The only flags that are printed, and for which there is the necessary machinery, are small Union Jacks. All other flags for all countries are painted."[1] The sketch in the De La Rue's Archives provided by Campbell might basically be considered approval from Hart during its production process.

The 1877 official contact between the Chinese Customs and England's Thomas De La Rue & Co. for stamp production originated from Hart's vision of establishing a national postal system in China. This all began with a March 5, 1877 letter of enquiry from Detring. As a result, De La Rue submitted a detailed, confidential technical report, detailing items such as specifically designed postage stamps,

---

1 Chen Xiafei and Han Rongfang chief ed., *Archives of China's Imperial Maritime Customs: Confidential Correspondence between Robert Hart and James Duncan Campbell, 1874 —1907*, Vol. I, p.35, 1990, Foreign Languages Press, Beijing.

postage envelope, sketches of postage emblems, design sketch of watermark, etc., to the Chinese Customs but failed to gain its approval. The collaboration between the two parties finally came to a halt after receipt of the instruction from Hart. Nonetheless, De La Rue played a vital role in the Chinese Customs officials' exploratory process for printing stamps. Their confidential report was essential and definitely regarded as a valuable reference for the Chinese Customs. Although De La Rue was not selected by the Chinese Customs as a partner for its postage stamp production, China's pace for creating national postal services had not been set aside. The curtain for staging our self-produced Large Dragons was opened slowly, but surely.

Zhao Yue

June 2018

德纳罗设计图稿

德纳罗 1877 年中国档案

英国德纳罗公司[1]1877 年中国档案，现保存于英国皇家邮政博物馆。本书对该档案内容及图片的使用得到了英国皇家邮政博物馆的许可。

---

1 英国著名的货币印制商和纸张制造商，始创于 1813 年。

德纳罗设计图稿

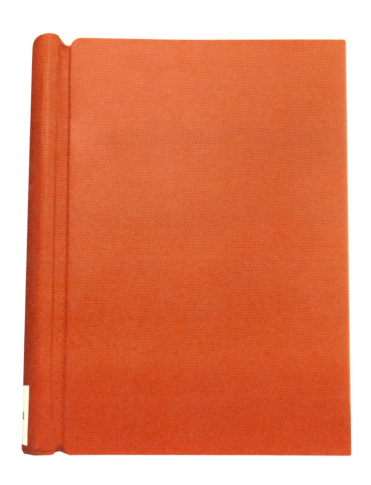

德纳罗为中国海关设计的纸张水印图稿

1877 年 6 月 8 日 [1] 德纳罗公司致金登干函附件 J 的一部分，
原附件在图稿的上方标注："推荐给中国邮票所用纸张的水印图稿。"

（图片提供：Interasia Auctions）

1　此日期为德纳罗公司撰文的原始日期，后根据金登干的要求修改为 6 月 18 日。

德纳罗设计图稿

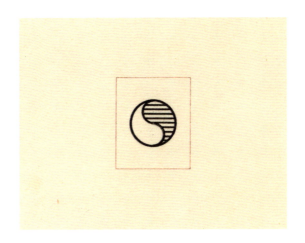

德纳罗为中国海关设计的邮票图稿

1877 年 6 月 8 日德纳罗公司致金登干函附件 J 的一部分，

原附件在图稿的上方标注："推荐给中国邮票之备选图稿，其面值系属假设。"

1958 年英国皇家集邮协会出版的《德纳罗英国及海外邮票史（1855—1901）》

（*The DE LA RUE HISTORY of BRITISH & FOREIGN POSTAGE STAMPS, 1855 to 1901*）一书中刊登了这两幅设计稿的图片。

（图片提供：Interasia Auctions）

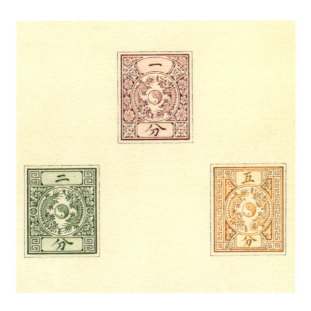

1955 年附件 J 的展页

为附件 J 在 1955 年"德纳罗公司印制邮票一百周年展览"中的展页,展页上方标注:"1877 年,我们与中国海关税务司金登干[1]先生接洽,他来自大清帝国海关总税务司署伦敦办事处,我们向他提交了一份有关印刷邮票的方案。附件 J 于 1877 年 6 月 18 日提交。"2014 年英国皇家集邮协会出版的《德纳罗藏集》(*The De La Rue Collection*)一书中刊登了此页。

(图片提供:英国皇家邮政博物馆)

---

1 金登干(James Duncan Campbell, 1833-1907 年),苏格兰人。关于金登干在中国海关驻伦敦办事处的职务,德纳罗公司使用的是 Commissioner,系金登干名片上所印之职务,实际职务为"Non-Resident Secretary",通常称为"主任"。本书翻译时,在使用 Commissioner 时译为"税务司",使用 Secretary 时译为"主任"。

德纳罗设计图稿

CHINA

In 1877 we were approached by Mr. James D.
Campbell, Commissioner of Customs, China, from
the London Office of the Inspectorate General of
Chinese Imperial Maritime Customs, to submit a
proposal for printing stamps. Appendix J was
submitted on June 18, 1877 together with Appendix
A on the next page.

Appendix I

*Sketch of the watermark to be made in the paper
employed for the proposed Postage Stamps for China.*

*Alternative sketches of the proposed Postage Stamps
for China the duties are merely suppositions.*

*Engraver's proofs of Adhesive stamps with
an animal or a bird in the centre.*

93

1955 年附件 A 的展页

与附件 J 一起在 1955 年"德纳罗公司印制邮票一百周年展览"中展出。附件 A 展示了德纳罗公司用凹版、平版、压花和凸版工艺所印制的邮票。下方为中国海关 1878 年发行的大龙邮票一套,以反映德纳罗公司在 1877 年为中国海关筹印邮票时所作出的探索和努力。2014 年英国皇家集邮协会出版的《德纳罗藏集》一书中刊登此页。

(图片提供:英国皇家邮政博物馆)

Specimens submitted to the Inspector General
of Chinese Imperial maritime Customs in London
on June 18, 1877 with a proposal for printing
stamps for China.

0000503

Appendix A 18 June 77

Intaglio printed stamps

Lithographic printed stamp

Embossed stamps

Surface printed stamps

1878 - 83
Specimens of the actual stamps typographed by
the Customs Statistical Department, Shanghai
for the initial Chinese issue.

CHINA & SHANGHAI.

95

德纳罗为中国海关设计的邮资信封

1877 年 6 月 8 日德纳罗公司致金登干函附件 I 的一部分，信封的上方标注："推荐给中国之邮资信封样品，一只展示正面，另一只为背面。"

（图片提供：赵建先生）

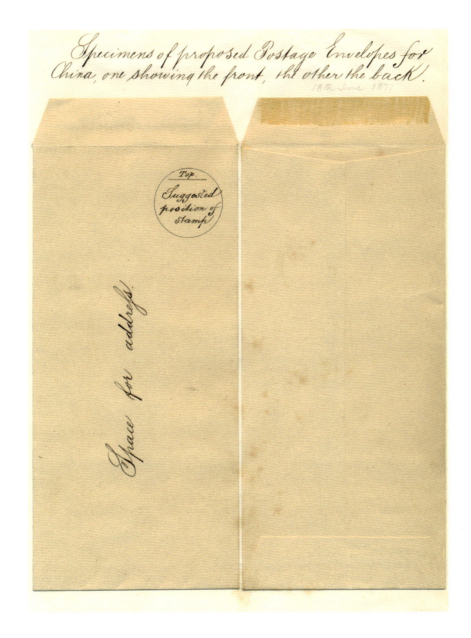

Specimens of proposed Postage Envelopes for China, one showing the front, the other the back.

18th June 1897

Top.
Suggested position of Stamp

Space for address.

德纳罗为中国海关设计的邮资信封邮资符图稿

与邮资信封设计图稿均系属 1877 年 6 月 8 日德纳罗公司致金登干函附件 I。

（图片提供：赵建先生）

德纳罗设计图稿

德纳罗档案中留存的附件 I 复印件

德纳罗档案中保存的附件 I 复印件，邮资符图稿上方标注："为上面邮资信封推荐的压印邮资符图稿。"

（图片提供：英国皇家邮政博物馆）

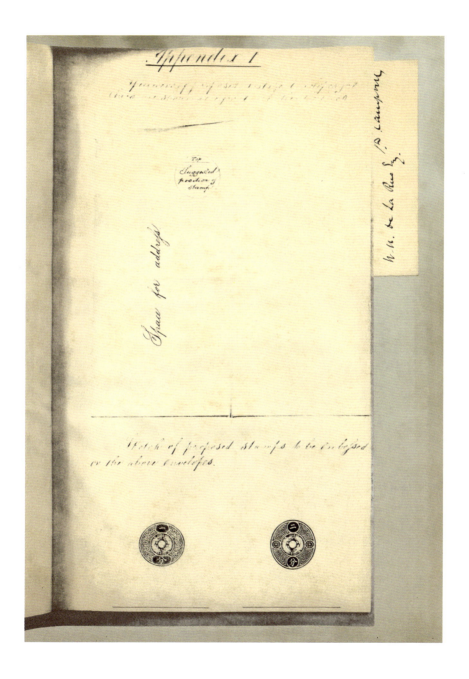

中文译本

1877 年 5 月 1 日中国海关的询函[1]

1. 在英国印制一百万枚邮票，开销几何？（50-60 英镑[2]）

2. 采购机器设备和纸张在中国每周印制一百万枚邮票，耗资几许？（设想而已[3]）

3. 如基本辅助劳力皆在中国就地雇佣，每周印制一百万枚邮票，英国雇员每月所需的用度几多？（将会出具详尽报告[4]）

黄色	御用之色
红色和粉色	欣悦
蓝色	哀伤
绿色	欣悦
棕色	哀伤[5]

---

1 此询函粘贴在德纳罗 1877 年中国档案的第一页。1877 年 3 月 5 日，德璀琳曾致函金登干，就印制邮票提出了三个问题，参见《清末天津海关邮政档案选编》，中国集邮出版社 1988 年版，第 21 页。5 月 1 日，此三个问题转询德纳罗公司，原件无抬头及书写人姓名，从笔迹看，非德璀琳和金登干书写。此份文件的左下角贴有金登干名片。

2 在原件中用铅笔标注，似为德纳罗公司所为。

3 同上。

4 同上。

5 五种颜色及其说明在原件中用铅笔标注，似为德纳罗公司所为。

1877 年 5 月 22 日金登干致德纳罗函 [1]

大清帝国海关

总税务司署伦敦办事处

斯托里门 8 号，圣詹姆斯公园，西南区

1877 年 5 月 22 日

阁下 [2]：

随函附奉我早前所收来自北京的两幅画稿。

"阴阳"图案中，阴面应该朝上 。我还寄给了您一张大尺幅的"龙"图。

烦请能在下一个寄件日（星期五）前给我报告，我已于上周五电告中国资料即将备妥。

金登干

谨上

1　1877 年 5 月 24 日信函归档至 W.W.D.（即 W.W. 德纳罗先生），档号：Fol261Vo.18。
2　没有注明信件呈送对象，根据前后内容分析，收信人应该是 W.W. 德纳罗先生。

又及：方案拟妥，烦将两张小画稿归还。

金登干

1877 年 5 月 23 日金登干致德纳罗函 [1]

斯托里门 8 号，圣詹姆斯公园，西南区

1877 年 5 月 23 日

阁下 [2]：

昨天寄奉贵司的两张小画稿中，各有一个悬浮在中的球体，即所谓"阴阳"。

金登干

谨上

1　1877 年 5 月 24 日信函归档 W.W.D.，档号：Fol261Vo.18。
2　没有注明信件呈送对象，根据前后内容分析，收信人应该是 W.W. 德纳罗先生。

1877 年 6 月 8 日备忘录

1877 年 6 月 8 日

备　忘

5 月 3 日与金登干先生第二次晤谈，我向他解释，我司以往只与英国的商办做生意，由此为与中国政府直接交易仍踌躇未决。他告知，其交付我司的每笔订单，将由丽如银行备妥并作资金担保。

W.W. 德纳罗[1]

1　指沃伦·威廉·德纳罗（Warren William De La Rue），德纳罗公司创始人托马斯·德纳罗（Thomas De La Rue，1793—1866）之孙，其父威廉·德纳罗（William De La Rue，1815—1889）是托马斯·德纳罗的长子。他生意上非常敬业，同时又是纽马克特一位精明的赛马主。

1877 年 6 月 8 日德纳罗致金登干函

机密

> 布伦希尔街 110 号，
>
> 伦敦，中东区，
>
> 1877 年 6 月 8 日 [1]

阁下：

您最近收到的来自中国海关总税务司的备忘录，连同您的电报答复，均已收悉。为履行承诺，承蒙俯允，我们将逐步向您提供所需资料，以便完成《有关背胶邮票项目报告》的上呈。

此函将主要聚焦于邮政服务所使用的邮票，这亦是您最为眷注之所在，当然，经您应允，我们将在此函结尾时介绍有关税务、海关或法律票证的详情，并说明适用条件。

背胶邮票有四种不同的印制方式，即，

（A）凹版印刷工艺（the intaglio printing process）；

（B）平版印刷工艺（the lithographic printing process）；

（C）压花工艺（the embossing process），通常与其他印刷工艺

---

1 原件中曾将此日期用铅笔划去，并在左侧注明："金登干先生将此日期修改为 18 日，见他 1877 年 6 月 29 日的信函。"档案中未见该函。德纳罗公司在 1955 年展览此函附件 A 与附件 J 的说明中使用的日期为 6 月 18 日。

结合使用；

（D）凸版印刷工艺（the surface-printing process）。

我们将按照上述顺序介绍这些工艺，切入正题之前需要说明一下，附件所列出的各种邮票票样，特意加盖了"Cancelled"戳以示作废。

（A）在凹版印刷工艺中，邮票图案借助于称之为"雕刻刀"的刀形器械刻在钢模上。譬如，我们拟用此种工艺印制字母 A。首先，要将构成这个字母的线条刻或刮到钢模上，深度相当于书写纸厚度。接下来，用熟亚麻籽油混合所需各色颜料（比如蓝色、红色、绿色、黄色等等）调成印刷油墨，用碎布蘸染油墨涂于模具之上，使模具表面涂满油墨并且在凹处形成字母 A。然后，用干净的碎布在模具上来回擦拭，去除表面的油墨，嵌入凹槽的油墨则不受影响。这样，除了雕刻的字母 A 填满了油墨，模具表面非常干净，显而易见，如果可以将油墨从模具凹槽处转移到纸张表面，就能印出字母 A。其方法是将一张纸放在模具上，然后将两者一并置于相互作用的滚筒中间，通过较大的外力在模具上挤压纸张。较金属而言，油墨对纸张更具亲和力，只要纸张充分受压接触模具，就会吸附凹槽中的油墨，将纸张从模具上移开，油墨也就附着其上，而不会复存于凹槽之中。此为凹版印刷工艺之概要。不难理解，同样的道理不仅适用于印刷一个简单的字母 A，而且适合于一串较为复杂的字符，如同附件 A 最上部所展示的凹版印刷邮票，每条线纹都代表着印版上的一处凹槽。

当然，邮票不是单枚而是成组地印制。在我们国家，由于英镑拥有 240 个货币单位（也就是便士），因此每个印张有多达 240 枚邮票。此外，240 枚邮票一个印张，其尺寸大小也非常便于印制。需要理解的是，这 240 枚邮票，不需要用只有一枚邮票图案的印模或印版在纸张的不同位置上单独压印 240 次，而是用一个拥有多枚邮票子模的印版印出，其数量和一个印张上的邮票相一致。然而，雕版师仅需雕刻一枚邮票图案即可。他所做的小版或小模称为母模，是用于印制 240 枚邮票的全尺寸印版的母版。印刷用版是以母模借助于某种设备复制而成，这种设备缺少图示很难描述。简而言之，低碳钢辊在巨大的压力之下反复轧过母模，直到辊子上的金属被挤压进模具的凹槽之中，于是母模的凹槽被精确地复制在钢辊表面。钢辊加热烧红再投入冷水硬化，加压轧过一块钢板即可得一个母模的摹版，因为钢辊上的凸纹在受压之下可以在印版上产生相应的压痕。用这种方法不仅可以从钢辊上拓得一个压痕，而且可以通过重复操作获取任意数量，前提是钢辊保持良好的状态。由于钢辊在使用之前被加工至极高的硬度，因此也不用担心磨损。即便有所损耗，也可以用母模再翻制一个新的钢辊，简单至极。这样，我们掌握了复制一定数量母模摹版的方法，借助于特定工具，就能制作出间距相同的 240 枚或少于 240 枚邮票的金属印版。

（B）至于平版印刷工艺，母模的制备方法与凹版印刷完全相同，但印版制作与上述方式不同，其图案是从"转印纸"（transfer paper）上获得的。转印纸是在普通纸的表面预先上浆，以便形成可溶的薄层。印稿绘制在薄层上，在没有干透时，正面朝下贴到一块光滑的印版石上。印版石对印刷油墨这类油性物质有亲和力，印稿贴上去后，印版石会吸附所接触的油墨。当然，不仅要使印稿接触到印版石，还要将其从纸上转印到印版石上。纸张的背面要稍作润湿，这样表面的可溶薄层能受到水的作用。当纸张充分湿润时，就用一种特殊的按压方式把它用力压在印版石上。于是，纸张与印版石紧密接触，可溶薄层从纸张上脱离，由此油墨被剥离，牢固地吸附在印版石上。这样，我们就得到一块表面有印稿的具有一定渗透性的多细孔印版石，印稿油性、斥水，对印刷油墨有亲和力。如果用一块含水的海绵拂过印版石，没有印稿的部分会吸收水分，而有印稿的部分则会排斥水分。用一个涂满印刷油墨（由熟亚麻籽油和颜料调成）的滚筒滚压过湿润的印版石，印刷油墨就会吸附在图案上，而其中的空白处则受水拒墨。需要说明的是，印版石用于印刷之前，上面的转印图稿还需用酸性溶液加以固化，使其牢牢附着于印版石之上，印刷才能不损丝毫。以上述方式将一层印刷油墨刷到图案上时，只需将一张纸覆在印版石上并对其按压，便能获得一件印刷成品。通过这种方法，纸张与印版石的表面紧密接触，依靠滚筒将图案上的印刷油墨覆压到纸上，当纸从印版石上揭下来时，所需的图稿便跃然其上。附件 A 中我们提供了通过这种方法印制的邮票票样，以作例证。

由此可见，只需用转印纸从母模上获得必要数量的单个图稿，并将它们排成彼此合适的间距覆在印版石上，然后按上述方法弄湿转印纸的背面，便能制成一个 240 枚或其他数量邮票的印版。同理，任何数量的邮票都可以像处理一枚邮票那样转印到印版石上。

（C）如前所述，印制邮票的压花工艺通常与某种印刷工艺相结合。由于我们正在分别探讨几种印刷工艺，所以在此不考虑这些印刷工艺是如何应用于邮票压花，因为只要理解了这些印刷工艺，清楚压花之前已使用了何种印刷工艺，便可充分描述印制压花的方法。在附件 A 中可以看到压花邮票的票样，通常压花位于邮票图案的中部，图案的其余部分则是印制出来的。当然，如果想要批量压花，也不费事儿。过程如下：用淬火的钢制工具在一块低碳钢块或模具上雕刻图案，完工后，用上述第一种工艺中描述的方法将模具硬化，即可用邮票大小的方形铅块从模具上拓得图案。借助于螺旋压力机，这种专用工具可以使铅块即使承受挤压入钢模凹槽的强大压力，也能保持精确的方形，从而制成一个完美的子模。由此，以同样的方式压制成 240 个或与印版所需数量一致的铅模，然后将它们精确地排列在一起，去除印版上凹陷部分的铅块毛刺，便组成了一块所需印版的精确副版。将排好的铅模副版放置在一个电池槽内，通过电铸工艺制出铜质副版。铜质副版从铅模上拆下，就成为印版，印版实际上包含了铅质母模的许多精确子模。先将其固定在一块铁板上，然后置于强力螺旋压力机之下，上面垫上一层厚软的杜仲橡胶。压力机开始工作，通过对杜仲橡胶重复击打，将其压入印版的凹槽内。当杜仲橡胶被强行嵌入版模的每一个凹槽时，取出杜仲橡胶，将其固定在印版所对应的螺旋压力机的上模座上。给已经印好的邮票印张压花，先将印张正面朝下放在印版上，在压力机的强力挤压下，杜仲橡胶与上模座一起下落，将纸张压进印版的每个凹陷处。把印张从印版上取出正面朝上时，会发现那些压进印版里的凸起部分之厚度与凹槽深度成正比。

现在，这三种印制邮票的工艺都存在非常大的争议，不仅是因为它们缺乏改良，操作不便，更重要的是所印制的邮票不仅能被伪造，而且可以擦除销戳，遮人耳目地二次使用。先例显示，使用凹版印刷工艺，油墨会在纸上留下凸纹，且油墨未干时这些凸纹非常明显，尽管它们在干燥过程中随着油墨收缩会变得平坦一些，显然邮票的印刷部分一定会比纸张表面高出一些（虽然肉眼很难察觉这种差异），这是由于填充在印版凹槽中的印刷油墨以凸纹的形式印在了纸张之上。这种情况对作伪者极为有利，由于有凸纹，就可以用下面的方式制作与印版一模一样的仿品。先准备好蚀刻底料石蜡和沥青，在钢板或铜板表面涂上薄薄的一层并干化。将待处理的凹版邮票面朝下放在印版有涂料的那一面，两者一起经过一对压辊，其作用是把图案的凸纹压进蚀刻涂料，涂料较脆，所以能被压陷。然后用酸液处理印版，侵蚀蚀刻底料被压陷部位的金属，从而产生一个完整的图案，换而言之，金属印版上没有凸纹压陷之处，可以免受酸液的腐蚀。实际上，可以把凹版邮票的凸纹视同刀刃，用其刻穿印版的保护层，从而将酸液要腐蚀的部位暴露出来。因此，虽然（纸张上的）凸纹不能在金属印版上压出凹纹，但可以通过介质间接地获得凸纹对应的纹路，等同于复制了印刷品的原始印版。伪版凹纹的深度取决于酸液留存的时间长短。如我们所展示的那样，以这种方式生产凹版邮票印版的复制品，效果非常好，足以乱真。

这种作伪手段只适用于凹版印刷的邮票，因为只有凹版印刷才会产生油墨的凸纹效应。对此，我来解释一下，在平版和凸版印刷工艺中，油墨仅仅印在纸张表面，薄薄的一层，视觉上不会感到厚度增加。然而，平版印刷工艺非常不适合邮票印刷，因为图案必然会模糊不清或者产生污痕，达不到分明和清晰的效果，而这对于防伪至为紧要。除此以外，用此工艺印刷的邮票与用凹版工艺印刷一样，甚至更易伪造。转印工艺在作伪中的成功取决于快干油墨所具有的某些特性，其中一种成分（亚麻籽油）可以用作印刷油墨。印刷油墨暴露在空气中会变硬，异常干燥，只有浸泡在稀盐酸溶液中才能恢复到原有的黏稠状态。将一份干燥的印刷品以此方式处理，它便会具备类似于首次印刷的状况。将其置于印版石上，然后施力，油墨软化后就会黏附，经熟练技工细致操作，足以使印版石上的图稿达到适合印刷的条件。此即通过转印进行作伪的惯常手法，但另有一种更为精练而实用的工艺，可以制作出相当精准的凹版或平版邮票的复制品。只要印版石上有一个良好的图案，平版印刷工人能够生产出与凹版印刷类似的制品，当然也可以根据印版石上的特定图稿，以其他印刷技术来复制原版邮票。在此工艺中，其实我们利用的不是油墨的性能，而是油墨在稀盐酸作用下产生油性物质而具备亲和性特点。现将邮票浸泡在一杯水里，持续浸泡直至沉入杯底，而水也沁入了纸内。水面会上浮一层油花，用镊子将邮票正面朝上打斜地穿过油层取出，由于湿纸不粘油，纸张表面的印刷油墨上便形成一个油层。于是，空白部位非常干净，而印刷部位上则沾有一层油墨，可以很容易地转印到印版石上，因为油有足够的亲和力，可以轻易地附着在印版石上，从而制作出一个可以用来印刷的完美图稿。

在压花工艺中，作伪者会面临比凹版或平版印刷相对较易的工艺。操作手法是，在邮票底下放一块熟石膏或其他适用的材料，先获取一个翻模，再翻铸成金属母模。这样就可以轻而易举地通过电铸工艺或其他方法获取子模，且可以制造出印刷全张所需的任何数量。

除了已经发现的工艺本身的缺陷，还有另外两个因素制约以上工艺的使用，第一是不能使用"易褪色"（fugitive）油墨印刷邮票。第二是用这些工艺印制的邮票易被伪造不说，其品相也有瑕疵。考虑到第一点提到的缺陷，我们会暂缓使用凹版印刷工艺；同时，我们应该指出，凹版印刷邮票外观粗糙，既不清晰也不耐用，因为凸纹上的油墨会由于磨损而形成污迹，这在印制邮票时会频繁发生，绝不比邮递过程中少。如前所述，平版印刷邮票的质量十分低劣。而压花邮票不仅本身有些粗糙，且由于凸起的缘故，较之其他工艺更松厚，很容易被压平。

（D）出于所有这些考虑，我们已不再使用上述三种工艺，而是选择三十年前成功完成的改良型凸版邮票印刷工艺，如附件 A 中的最后一组邮票所示。现在，这种工艺其实已经应用于我们印制的几乎所有邮票，从而使邮票免遭仿造，并且可以防止诈洗而被再次使用。这种工艺可以称之为反向的凹版工艺，因为母模中的图案不是刻成凹版，而是雕成凸版的。印版石或工作板由这种凸模制成，与上述压花印版非常相似，当然最终获得了一块带有凸纹而不是凹纹的印版。印制时用一种涂有"易褪色"印刷油墨的特殊滚筒经过印版，滚筒所接触的部分（即凸纹）被涂上一层薄薄的油墨。当纸张放在涂有油墨的印版上并受到压力（压力较大，由特种印刷机所产生），油墨就从印版转移到纸上，从而印制出精美的图案。由于母模极为精致，印版可以在纸上印出完美图案，用这种方式印刷的图案和纸张在同一平面上，没有凹版印刷邮票产生的凸纹。所以，凸版印刷的邮票不仅外观精致（这一点至关重要），而且通过印制图案的改良，使其免受作伪工艺的危害。邮票的性质越完善，便越能通过采用绘稿、雕刻或其他类似的工艺避免仿造，其具有较高品相的价值立刻凸显。事实上，即便作伪者拿到完美品相的邮票，连同仿制设备一起交给熟练的技师，也无法生产出高仿邮票，因为前述任何一种作伪方法都无法发挥作用。

以下，我来谈谈"易褪色"油墨的使用条件。这种油墨被称为"易褪色"，是因为它在去除邮票上的销盖戳记的溶剂作用下会褪色或消失，也就是说可溶于碳氢化合物等液体。凹版与平版印刷工艺不允许使用这样的油墨，所以由这两种工艺印制的邮票不受上述液体的影响，从而可以在干燥后长时间浸泡在汽油（被公认为是最方便清洁邮票的溶剂）中而不会发生任何明显的变化。邮票可以用手盖的方式销盖，这样的戳记标示在附件 B 的上部。这种用途的油墨有一个特殊的称呼叫"批注"（endorsing）油墨，干燥后具有几乎不溶于汽油的特性。据此，如果用"批注"油墨给一张用"易褪色"油墨印刷的邮票销戳，要洗掉销盖戳记就会损坏邮票，参见附件 B所示。第二份样品是一枚用"批注"油墨销戳的英国 3 便士邮票，后面跟了一枚同样被销了戳的邮票，但被用汽油处理过。如附件所示，邮票已经损坏，而销盖戳记只被洗掉一点点。因此，如果用"易褪色"油墨印制邮票，就可以用销盖戳记有效地销盖，邮票不能被清洗而二次冒用。而当邮票用了非易褪色油墨，如附件 B 的凹版印刷邮票所示，这两枚邮票用普通印刷油墨印制，下面一枚邮票的销盖戳记几乎被完全清除，而邮票没有受到影响。可以想见在以汽油处理之前，这枚邮票与上面的一枚外观完全相同。最重要的是，邮票应该用"易褪色"油墨印制，这样的话，销盖戳记会是一种高效的注销方式。

如前所言，这种戳记通常依靠手盖，但当需要处理大量信件时，我们可以提供一种销戳机，类似于附件 C 上部顶端的照片所示，这种机器（手动操作）比较便宜，价格只有 12 英镑（不包括包装等费用），一天可以销盖大量的邮戳。它可销盖一枚邮戳或双工戳，如附件 C 和 D 的图片所示。在双工戳里，其中一把邮戳用机密符号或者组合字母销盖邮票，以标示局所，而边上的另一把邮戳销盖信封，不但可以反映城镇地名，而且显示销盖的时间和日期。后者不能独立销盖，确切地说，它只是邮戳的附戳。从某种意义而言，这是销盖戳记最重要的部分，即日期。为此，双工戳上有四个钢制的字钉，最上面的字钉代表小时，其他三个字钉分别表示日、月和年。邮戳的端头以特别的方式拧开是为了方便装入字钉，每当需要时可以随意更换。双工戳名副其实，即包括邮票销盖戳及其附戳，它是专为英国设计的，能否适用别处，尚不确定。我们倾向于使用一个含地名和日期的邮戳，如附件 D 下部的草图所示。

当邮戳不在机器上使用时，可以装上手柄，如上文提到的图片中所示。不难看出，这个手柄的顶部有三个孔。当只用一个邮戳时，使用中间的孔。当两个邮戳一起使用时，使用外侧的两个孔。

再回过头来考虑油墨的问题，我们应该指出，虽然使用"易褪色"油墨的主要目的是使邮票能够防伪而不被多次冒用，使用这种油墨的另一个突出优点，就是不能通过转印工艺去复制邮票，而转印工艺，如我们所说，适用于复制其他方法印制的邮票。采用转印工艺复制邮票，需被仿制的邮票原件使用油性油墨印制，由于"易褪色"油墨没有油性，所以不能用于这一工艺。因为当"易褪色"油墨泡在稀盐酸中时，不会膨胀变得黏稠，而且在使用我们所述的其他相关方法复制邮票时也不受油。简而言之，普通印刷油墨不适合邮票印制，而"易褪色"油墨则安全没有这些缺点。由此我们得出结论，用最佳工艺（即凸版印刷工艺）印制邮票绝对可以防伪，尤其能避免用我们所介绍的转印工艺进行复制。而平版印刷工艺生产的邮票，与凸版工艺相比还不够精致。

至此，我们只提及了邮票，现在将尽可能简短地解释一下税务、海关和法律票品所适用的条件。在使用邮票的情况下，销盖戳记均由邮局人员操作，一般使用我们前面所描述的那种手盖邮戳，但对于必须在各种文件上使用的票品，由于文件千差万别，销盖票品的任务通常便移交到了使用者的肩上。但是期望每个人按照要求在文件上粘贴票品，然后再提供所需的合适销盖戳记是不太现实的，这样的票品几乎必然是用笔简单地划销。所以，用笔划销的油墨必须与印制邮票的油墨完全不同，印制邮票的油墨只是在那些用作溶解销盖戳印的液体作用下才会褪色。而印制税务等票品时，使用的油墨必须能在去除用笔划销的溶液中褪色。尽管如此，虽然用笔划销可以使这些票品按规定作废，但在某些情况下，使用印戳来销盖这些票品也很方便（例如，在法庭上，手盖戳通常伸手可及）。因此，为了充分防伪，印制这类票品的油墨不仅要在溶解用笔划销试剂时褪色，而且还要在去除销盖戳印时也褪色。这种需求使得"双褪色"（doubly fugitive）的油墨投入了使用，我们在印制税务、海关和法律票品时所使用的油墨便是这种。我们只有三种"双褪色"油墨，票样在附件 E 中。附件最上端的邮票是用淡紫色"双褪色"油墨印制的，这种颜色一般用于印制低面值的票品，而较高面值的则是通过印刷成绿色和深紫色来加以区别，如下图票样所示。这三种"双褪色"颜色可以参阅我们上面提及的附件，在没有销盖的票品旁边，我们为每种情况提供了两枚销盖票品的票样，一枚用笔划销，另一枚用戳销盖。每一种情况下，我们都用草酸去除用笔划销的痕迹，并用苯消除邮戳销盖的痕迹。如图所示，前者破坏了票品的颜色，使之无法修复，而后者则洗去了票品的主图。在每一种情况下，用戳销盖比用笔划销的票品更加难洗去。税务、海关和法律的票品是用"双褪色"油墨印刷的，而邮票则是用"单褪色"（singly fugitive）油墨印刷的，区别仅此而已。这两类票品的防伪和印制条件如出一辙，只是前者比后者的印制难度更高。这在使用绿色和深紫色时尤为明显，因为它们是通过特殊工艺加工的，稳定性差，以致不能在受潮或粗暴处理的情况下使用，因为它们碰到水或刮擦会立即受损。因此，当税务、海关或法律票品面对磨损问题时，印制时唯一可用颜色是淡紫色，如附件 E 的上部所示。这种颜色具有我们所描述的"双褪色"特性，其色牢度与"单褪色"油墨在邮票印制中相同。

谈及印花税票，可以留意一下印度政府所采用的一种特殊的票品形式。他们发现，规定大多数法律文书使用"印花纸"（Stamped Paper）很方便，这种"印花纸"由带水印的纸页组成，抬头印有精美的印花。如果文书的内容超出了"印花纸"内的空间范围，则把普通纸裁切成起始页"印花纸"的大小接续使用。由于可以防伪，这种"印花纸"值得大力推荐。我们的附件 L 上有其中一种税额的样张，但在印度有 100 种以上的税额，所有图案均独一无二。

在讲述了印制背胶邮票各种条件和工艺之后，有必要详细介绍一下通行的工艺是如何运用的，以及政府部门在管控方面采取了哪些预防措施。因此，以下我们接着谈谈 1 令邮票（500 张）的整个生产过程。

每类邮票所使用的纸张都有专用的水印，这种水印不仅从一开始就给作伪者设置了障碍，能够进一步防伪，而且由于邮票必须使用特种纸张印刷，还起到了管控目的。附件 F 最上部的样例是一张刚从造纸机印出来的带有水印的邮票纸，这仅是我们为不同类型的邮票所生产的众多种类中的一种，每个种类都有不同的水印。水印辊（用于生产水印纸的专用设备）由一名政府官员保管在保险库内，只有当需要生产特种纸张时才会被取出。在纸张生产的整个过程中都有一名官员寸步不离，并且一完工就将水印辊还回保险库。还要说明一下，有两名官员常年负责管理着我们邮票用纸的生产加工，并且兼管库存。这样，他们可以不时地分发所需纸张，并在出库前一张一张地仔细清点数量。每次交付，他们都登记在册。在纸张交给我方前会再次核对数量，我方第三次确认数量正确之后，会向当局提交一张收据，通过必要的流程来为邮票的印制做好准备。在刷胶过程中，纸张背面的刷胶量应使邮票牢固地粘贴在信封上。附件 F 下边的示例和上边的示例裁切于同一张纸，在经过上述工艺之后非常光滑。纸张被送到印刷部门，由政府官员负责看管。接收之前会仔细清点，以确保正确数量的纸张入库，并在专用簿上记下数量。印刷过程在政府官员的现场监督下进行，事实上官员管理着整个库房、库房内使用的设备及其主要部件，例如印版和模具，他们出于安全考虑，会在夜间以及周末和节假日里将其存放在库房（防火防盗）里。实际上，有至少 40 名政府人员在我们公司从事着监督工作，说明这里有严格的管控体系，我们每年生产的邮票总产值高达几百万英镑，毋庸置疑，业务量还会持续增长。

需要说明一下，我们为之服务的多国政府都有自己的管理人员，因此我们认为有必要为每个政府建立单独的印刷部门。与为英国政府供应全系列高价值邮票一样，我们也为印度及下述国家提供全套服务，显而易见，由我们印制的邮票具有广泛性。

由我们印制邮票的国家（和地区）

英国	安提瓜
印度	巴哈马群岛
巴巴多斯	尼维斯
百慕大群岛	圣·克里斯托弗
英属圭亚那	圣赫勒拿
英属洪都拉斯	圣卢西亚
好望角	塞拉利昂
锡兰	英属海峡殖民地
多米尼加	塔斯马尼亚
冈比亚	特立尼达拉
黄金海岸	维尔京群岛
香港	西澳大利亚
牙买加	奥兰治自由邦
拉各斯	新南威尔士
马耳他	南澳大利亚
毛里求斯	新西兰
蒙特塞拉特	维多利亚
纳塔尔	

以及许多其他外国政府

如上所言，为了达到监管目的，我们所服务的不同政府拥有各自独立的部门工作人员。不仅如此，每个印制部门采用与上述类似的控制体系，而且如前所述，主管官员在完全掌控所有的设备和物料的同时还监督生产，这样一来，还能防止工人从中揩油。实际上，这项工作几乎完全置于政府的管控之下，如同在政府衙署办公，而我们只负责实务操作。

蒙请暂置背胶邮票之议题，讨论一个我们认为中国政府可能感兴趣的问题，即邮资信封。如您所知，我们为英国及印度政府加工了大量的这种信封。在印度，它们不仅普惠大众，而且也让邮政官员受益良多，工作效率因使用了合适的信封而得以极大提高，在政府销售邮资信封之前，印度当地人使用的信封大多不结实。而邮资信封具有尺寸统一和字体工整的优点，与此前大小不一、形状各异的信封相比，处理起来容易些许。中国的情况可能有所不同，然而，我们认为一款合适的邮资信封可能会发挥很好的作用，因为在英国这里发行的邮资信封满足了实际需求，对于做事讲究的人来说，压花的邮资信封比粘贴邮票的信封更美观整洁，可以省去粘贴邮票的麻烦（这一点最为重要）。在附件 G 中，我们展示了一只为英国政府制作的邮资信封，在附件 H 中，展示了我们为印度所做的两个品种或面值的样品。我们估计，这些信封的年度消耗总量不少于五千八百万件，而且这个数字会与日俱增。邮票是通过精密的机器一次性压花并印制彩色背景的，使用压花工艺是因为这是唯一一种能以较快速度在信封上留下较好效果的方法。与压花背胶邮票一样，我们所讨论的邮资信封上的压花邮票也存在着类似的争议。由于给信封压上了一些难以复制的印记，事实上无疑具有了一定的防伪作用。作伪者很难找到我们所使用的特种纸张，即使找到，也会为如何逼真地仿制信封而犯愁。信封本身在某种程度上就难以模仿，当上面印上邮票时则愈加困难。事实上，虽然邮票的安全性未必尽如人意，但也从未收到过有关我们制作的邮资信封被仿制的任何重大投诉。

诚如阁下所言，附件 G 和 H 所示的英国和印度政府发行信封的具体样式不符合中国民众的需求。但附件 I 上的信封可能更合适一些。此型信封的裁切会比英国和印度信封浪费些纸张，但在其他方面几乎一样容易制作。邮票可以印在指定位置，或者任何其他可能需要的地方。在附件 I 的信封下面，我们提供了可能会用到的两种面值的压花邮票的图稿。图稿中有色部分代表背景，而白色或阴影位置显示那些显著凸起的部分。我们可以生产这样的信封，随信附了 24 只，费用大约是每千只十一先令。这一价格不包括 £65（六十五镑）的压花母模的费用和每种面值的模具 £40（四十镑）的费用，但包括印刷捆扎 24 只信封可能需要的包装带和内衬锡纸的箱子，以及免费送至伦敦码头装船的费用。

当然，我们不会拘泥于特定形状或规格大小的信封，而是可以在相应的价格下生产任何指定形式和纸张质量的信封，此外还可在上面运用压花工艺印刷所需图案或面值的邮票。

现在回过来探讨背胶邮票，恭请阁下留意一下附件 J 最上边的设计稿，我们考虑将其作为中国邮票用纸的水印。它由阴阳符号组成，但去除了圆点，因为我们无法使圆点在纸张上取得满意的效果。在附件 J 的水印设计之后，我们给出了两套或两种中国背胶邮票的设计。每种情况下的设计都采用了相同的主图，也就是双龙环抱着阴阳符号。在保留这些共性的同时，我们试图使邮票在可以自由发挥的有限图幅内不尽相同，因为最重要的是，一种面值的邮票应该明显有别于其他面值，不仅要防止二者相混淆，而且任何处理手段都不能使低面值邮票被误以为高面值邮票。举个例子，假设一分邮票在设计和颜色上与二分邮票相同，二者之间的唯一区别是汉字所示的面值，显而易见的是，中国的数字"一"会变成"二"，一分的邮票会变成其双倍的真实价值。例子虽然简单，但我们认为，这足以说明印制邮票要有所区别。实际经验告诉我们，区别越大越好。我们设计的尺寸参照了英国邮票的大小，这个尺寸非常值得采用，因为我们所有的设备适于印制标准尺寸的邮票（是最为合适的邮票尺寸），因此任何票幅或形状的改变都需要付出很大的代价。

当然，我们所讨论的设计只是手绘图，仅粗略地展示了成品邮票的外观。我们会对设计图进行精雕细刻，如附件 A 中的票样，或附件 J 底部雕刻师的黑色试模票，从中可以看出，我们能够把邮票做得极度精美，自然界中的任何动物都能处理得像英国邮票上的女王头像那样细腻。阴阳符号结合双龙会给我们的雕刻师相当大的施展空间。同时我们认为，如果有可能采用某种像龟一样的动物，或任何其他中国的代表动物作为中心装饰，邮票的成品效果可能会更讨人喜欢。不过，这完全是中国当局所考虑的问题。需要理解的是，附件 J 所给出的设计稿的面值仅仅是假设，对于任何可能需要进一步修改的字体，我们都很容易作出调整，我们的设计便于修改，能够印制任意面值。

假设需要在设计之后印制邮票，我们会制作一个有阴阳和双龙的母模。以此再制作三个含有相同图案的子模，在被我们选作一分银面值的子模上面雕刻设计其余部分。至于其他两个子模，一个将制成二分银面值，另一个则制成五分银面值。如果还需要子模，就可以用母模制作所需的数量，然后在上面雕刻合适的完整图案。通过这种方法，我们确保了每个子模或邮票（防伪问题的重要对象）的主要特征，虽然我们省去了在每种面值上雕刻的工时和花费，但我们并没有运用在母模上复制子模去生产不同面值的特殊办法，在此信中我们无法做出详细的描述。

按所描述的方式制成了不同面值的子模后，便将开始生产印版。一个龙图母模的价格为 £75（七十五镑），每种面值子模的价格为 £50（五十镑），全张 240 枚的每块印版为 £85（八十五镑），生产水印辊的价格为 £80（八十镑）。我们的邮票价格为每一百万枚 £54/3/4（五十四英镑三先令四便士）。这个价格包括内衬锡纸包装箱的伦敦离岸价格，也包括邮票刷胶和打孔的价格，如附件 K 所示的四分之一张 12 分香港邮票票样，这是基于将邮票印刷成每个全张 240 枚的假设。整个生产过程受类似我们为英国、印度或其他国家的政府生产的管控体系的监督。

关于您所提出在中国建厂印制邮票的成本问题，本应给您一些建议，但很抱歉，我们非常遗憾地表示，如果不知道每年生产的邮票数量，是无法做出费用估算的。同时实言相告，建立这样一套设施耗资巨大。事实上，我们觉得尝试实施此类计划是极不明智的，除非让邮政制度有一个适当的试运营，并要在英国组织系统的邮票生产。即使有可能在中国建立印制高品质邮票的工厂，眼下也无法满足工厂提出的新需求，因为别的不说，您会发现我们在这个问题上有不可或缺的丰富经验（我们的说法毫不夸张）。此外，没有大量的经费是不可能在中国建立和维持一支开展初步工作的员工队伍，而这些工作我们已经驾轻就熟。当然，我们的建议是，如果中国政府决定委托我们印制邮票，倘若首次的需求数量较小，他们应该请求英国政府或印度政府协助，来监控邮票的印制。当然，如果他们认为此法可行，我们非常乐意他们从自己国家派出一个或多个代表来监控生产。但在初始阶段邮票的需求量多半不会很大，在我们看来，（至少在初始阶段）尝试聘用现有的某位管理人员比较好，或者从你们办事处聘请一些助手来进行管控，因为通过此举中国政府同样可以获得绝对的安全，如同派用自己人管理生产。倘若邮票需求量不断增加，如果中国政府乐意的话，可以派自己的代表来管理，在这里组织和运转整个生产流程之后，他们才可以去考虑是否将生产转移到自己的国家。然而，经过深入的调研，我们倾向于相信，复杂的生产过程将使他们放弃在本国生产，我们确信，即使劝说最好的工人去中国，也不会生产出与我们同等质量的产品，且不说客观存在的气候问题，这可能会使印刷油墨和其他相关生产变得困难重重，没有我们的亲自监督，也必然使他们难以为继。我们不愿自我吹捧，也没向阁下夸大邮票生产中的巨大困难，这些困难只能通过我们长期经验积累及对业务的专心致志才能克服。我们认为，基于种种困难，在英国成千上万的印刷机构中，要生产出高质量的邮票，我们公司是不二之选。

中国当局应决定选择我司印制邮票。如果不认同我们的设计，不妨由中方提供设计图，我方来印制。如需不同面值的邮票，烦请寄来票面的汉字，用黑笔写在白纸或硬纸板上，字迹要清晰。字体写成一式两份或一式三份更佳。最好能估算出每种面值邮票或邮资信封的年消耗量。我们强烈建议首笔订单应该预订足以维持两到三年的用量（即一年的供应量用于使用，两年的供应量用作库存），借鉴印度的情况可以发现，始终保持两年供应量的库存十分必要，否则在我们补货前耗尽会相当麻烦。出现这种问题，部分是由于订单送抵我处时发生延误，部分是由于邮票繁琐的生产工序，部分是由于运输到印度的时间消耗。

烦请阁下拨冗阅函，亦望在您定夺之前，我方尽量言明细节，此函繁缛拖沓，万望海涵。

总之，我们对有关当局的垂青深表谢意。所需票样已随函附上，对阐明问题至关重要。

托马斯·德纳罗公司

谨上

致：金登干先生

斯托里门 8 号，西南区

1877 年 6 月 21 日金登干致德纳罗函 [1]

大清帝国海关

总税务司署伦敦办事处

斯托里门 8 号，圣詹姆斯公园，西南区

1877 年 6 月 21 日

阁下：

　　谨谢贵司之商录，我确信迟早会有机会向贵司订购一些中国当局所需物资。

金登干

谨上

致 W.W. 德纳罗先生

1　信函销盖德纳罗公司"1877 年 6 月 22 日收到 / 登记"戳。

中国海关总税务司署伦敦办事处订货单一

中国海关总税务司署伦敦办事处

订单号：　　　　　　　　　　　　申请编号：

　　　　　　　　　　...........................的投标

　　　　...............谨此提供最佳质量及制作的物品（以买方核查为准），

从订货日期起，可以确定的最短时间内，在 ....船上交货，

物品在下表中详细说明，每件物品单独报价，减掉所有的折扣和佣

金，加在一起总价 ....英镑。

　　　　　　　　　　签名：...

　　　　　　　　　　地址：...

　　　　　　　　　　日期：18........年........月........日

回函：主任[1]

　　斯托里门8号，圣詹姆斯公园，西南区

---

1 英文为 secretary，在档案中金登干的名片上使用的职务名称为 Commissioner of Customs China（中国海关税务司）。

物品详细描述：

  哈里尔德父子公司的新专利踏板式"布雷姆纳"平版印刷机，适合英式对开[1]尺寸，可手工操作。每台机器额外配备一个墨槽，大小合适，可随时更换。

数量：3 台

---

1 原文为 demy folio，demy 为英式纸张尺寸，大小为 22.5×17.5 英寸（517.5×444.5 毫米），demy folio 为其对开尺寸。

中国海关总税务司署伦敦办事处订货单二

中国海关总税务司署伦敦办事处

订单号：   申请编号：

..........................的投标

................谨此提供最佳质量及制作的物品（以买方核查为准），

从订货日期起，可以确定的最短时间内，在................船上交货，

物品在下表中详细说明，每件物品单独报价，减掉所有的折扣和佣

金，加在一起总价................英镑。

签名：..

地址：..

日期：18............年............月............日

回函：主任

斯托里门8号，圣詹姆斯公园，西南区

物品详细描述：

哈里尔德父子公司

品质上乘的改进型圆眼打孔机

宽度 25 英寸

如果一台机器可以每次打制一行以上的孔，则不再采购上述打孔机。附件是一页孔眼的精确尺寸和图案。

数量：2 台

中国海关总税务司署伦敦办事处订货单三

中国海关总税务司署伦敦办事处

订单号：　　　　　　　　　　申请编号：

　　　　　　　　　　..................的投标

　　　　..................谨此提供最佳质量及制作的物品（以买方核查为准），从订货日期起，可以确定的最短时间内，在..................船上交货，物品在下表中详细说明，每件物品单独报价，减掉所有的折扣和佣金，加在一起总价..................英镑。

　　　　　　　　　　签名：..................

　　　　　　　　　　地址：..................

　　　　　　　　　　日期：18........年........月........日

回函：主任

　　　斯托里门8号，圣詹姆斯公园，西南区

143

物品详细描述：

20 磅[1] 柠檬黄油墨

（见样本册 3 号）

20 磅 淡紫色油墨

（见样本册 15 号）

20 磅 巧克力色油墨

（见样本册 2 号）

20 磅 鳕鱼红油墨

（见样本册 13 号）

20 磅 翠绿色油墨

（见样本册 9 号）

10 磅 深桔黄油墨

（见样本册 5 号）

---

1 英制重量单位，1 磅约等于 0.454 千克。

中国海关总税务司署伦敦办事处订货单四

中国海关总税务司署伦敦办事处

订单号： 申请编号：

.........................的投标

.................谨此提供最佳质量及制作的物品（以买方核查为准），
从订货日期起，可以确定的最短时间内，在.........................船上交货，
物品在下表中详细说明，每件物品单独报价，减掉所有的折扣和佣
金，加在一起总价.........................英镑。

签名：...
地址：...
日期：18.........年.........月.........日

回函：主任

斯托里门 8 号，圣詹姆斯公园，西南区

物品详细描述：

　　手工纸 600 令，每令 500 张，适合印制附页尺寸和设计的邮票，每格之内均有旭日[1]水印。

　　上述纸张必须尽快发运，每批次 50 令。

数量：600 令

1　原文如此，应该指太极阴阳图案。

中国海关总税务司署伦敦办事处订货单五

中国海关总税务司署伦敦办事处

订单号：   申请编号：

                    ....的投标

            ....谨此提供最佳质量及制作的物品（以买方核查为准），

从订货日期起，可以确定的最短时间内，在 ....船上交货，

物品在下表中详细说明，每件物品单独报价，减掉所有的折扣和佣

金，加在一起总价 ....英镑。

                    签名：...

                    地址：...

                    日期：18........年........月........日

回函：主任

      斯托里门8号，圣詹姆斯公园，西南区

物品详细描述：

　　25 加仑[1] 邮票刷胶所使用的特制胶或合成胶，该胶需适应潮湿性气候条件。

　　上述产品必须每月分批供应 2 加仑。如果所需的配料能在中国混合的话，最好干燥后发运。

数量：25 加仑

1　英制体积单位，1 加仑约等于 4.55 升。

中国海关总税务司署伦敦办事处订货单六

中国海关总税务司署伦敦办事处

订单号：   申请编号：

                    ....的投标

            ....谨此提供最佳质量及制作的物品（以买方核查为准），

从订货日期起，可以确定的最短时间内，在 ....船上交货，

物品在下表中详细说明，每件物品单独报价，减掉所有的折扣和佣

金，加在一起总价 ....英镑。

                        签名：..

                        地址：..

                        日期：18.........年.........月.........日

回函：主任

        斯托里门 8 号，圣詹姆斯公园，西南区

物品详细描述：

最大号信件磅秤，与英国邮局所用同款。

数量：20 台

最小号信件磅秤，与英国邮局所用同款。

数量：30 台

每种磅秤均须配备万国邮联标准砝码（克重）。

1877 年 7 月 5 日金登干致德纳罗函[1]

大清帝国海关

总税务司署伦敦办事处

斯托里门 8 号，圣詹姆斯公园，西南区

1877 年 7 月 5 日

回函请提及 No.2475

并寄给中国海关办事处主任金登干

阁下：

关于我们昨天的谈话，现随函附上我发给总税务司的电报副本。

下一批来自中国的信函由于承载的法国轮船失事而随之灭失。我担心先前记录约定的备忘录、已查收的订单说明及其他有关资料都在这艘船上。否则，它们一定会在本月 16 日由英国邮政送达此地。

不管怎样，如果总税务司倾向于在中国而非在英国印制邮票，从我提请贵司审核的订单中，你或许对总税务司在上海设厂生产邮票有个基本了解，可以估算出在中国建厂所需之机械设备。

有基于此，可以考虑一下这些工艺中哪一种最适合上海的气候环境，以及充分利用海关造册处的现有资源。

---

1 信函 1877 年 7 月 6 日归档 W.W.D.，无归档号，归档戳记后用铅笔划去。

倘若总税务司回电报指示采购，我希望能提前作好准备，迅速发货。

金登干

谨上

致 W.W. 德纳罗先生

1877 年 7 月 5 日金登干致德纳罗函附件

7 月 4 日金登干发赫德的电报副本 [1]

"邮政订货单无法实施，机器、纸张和油墨皆不适用，详细报告已于 6 月 22 日寄出。您如立即寄来每种邮票的设计，收我汇报后再作电报指示，各种邮票可以在十周后送抵这里 [2] 交货，价格为每百万枚 54 英镑。先在这里印制，可保证有熟练的生产经验，节省时间并确保防伪——日后再向中国转产。"

1　此电译文亦载于《中国海关密档》(第八卷)，中华书局 1995 年版，第 120 页。此抄录副本与原电文略有不同。

2　即伦敦。

1877 年 7 月 5 日德纳罗致金登干函

布伦希尔街 110 号，中东区

1877 年 7 月 5 日

阁下：

关于本月 2 日您派给我司订购单中的机器和其他货品，我司不太愿意为此投标，因为在我们看来，这些与贵方需求完全不符，无法用于印制邮票。对于普通印刷而言，"布雷姆纳"平版印刷机是不错的机器，但如果用于印制邮票，则不仅动力不足，精度也差，总之它只适用于特定用途，即所谓"零散"印刷。

我们亦无意向您提供"哈里尔德"打孔机，相比之下"纳皮尔"机虽然价格稍高，但经验证明，其性能要比其他品牌优越甚多。同时，我们认为脚踏式打孔机根本不适合大批量邮票打孔，而必须使用英国政府在萨默耳特工厂所使用的机器。

贵方指定的油墨适用于普通印刷，绝不可用于邮票印制，因为一旦这种油墨变干，就可以在不损坏印刷图案的情况下清除表面的销盖戳记。因此，如果用这种油墨印刷邮票，即使全戳销盖，但很容易被洗去销印二次冒用，而不会露出破绽。所以，只能用"易褪色"油墨印制邮票，这一点至关重要。

所询之手工纸不适合邮票印刷，因为任何手工制作的纸张与精美印刷所需之纸张相去甚远。当我们最初印制邮票时，造纸机还没有达到现有的良好性能，那时（大概三四十年前），我们只好采用手工纸印制邮票，然而当能用机制纸获取效果不错的水印时，我们就立刻弃用了手工纸，因为手工纸的印刷总是差强人意，而且问题多多。除此之外，手工纸还无法保证厚度均匀，这也就是我们反对它用于特殊用途的另一原因，如果纸张厚薄不一，印刷品的外观就会千差万别，因为纸张的厚度超过了印刷机的调整范围，结果压得不是过轻就是过重，从而导致邮票色彩浓淡不一。现在，不仅要求邮票印刷精美，而且外观要高度一致，以便使用者可以轻松地辨识邮票真伪。

应该在印刷前将纸张的一面刷好背胶，这样就无需再配胶或使用合成胶，但我们担心如果将刷胶纸张发往中国，由于潮湿可能会产生不良影响，即使用衬锡的箱子包装也无济于事。

综上，我们认为，贵方想要订购的机器设备不适于邮票印制。当然，我们非常理解，在采购邮票印制设备时遇到的种种困难（由于对需要履行的特殊条款不熟悉的缘故），必须依赖订单拟定者的经验。而且在这种情况下，很难做出更佳的选择。

期冀中国政府能够借鉴我司在印制邮票方面的经验。在我们看来，为了提高信赖度，一国使用的邮票应该高度保真，此乃第一要务，如果质量不过硬，就会导致邮票在中国被任意伪造，依靠邮票营收的做法也必将受到质疑，鉴于所发行的邮票必须安全防伪，该体系势必会扩展到邮政业务以外的领域，这时大规模收费就会通过邮票代办来完成，像印度那样。这些观点理由充分，从印度可见一斑。大约三十年前，印度政府要印制邮票时，所咨询的第一家公司就是我们，其应用仅限于邮资业务。但从那时起，我们一直负责印制各种各样的印度邮票，当局亦岁入颇丰，毫无疑问，由于对邮票安全信心满满，邮政体系得以扩展，如果缺乏信心，那么它们的使用就会折回老路。我们之所以提到印度，是因为在我们看来，其国情与中国颇为类似——这两个国家的百姓都以善于仿制的耐心和技巧而著称[1]，当然英国和我们供应邮票的许多其他国家也面临同样的问题，除非在更为文明的地方，除了邮票本身具有防伪性外，政府亦严格审查，加强监管。固然，这并非不使用防伪邮票的理由，英国政府一直认为，从我司订制高品质邮票裨益良多。毋庸置疑，涉及兴办事宜，我们相信，这些观点及上月 18 日我们在信中深入探讨之内容[2]，将会说服当局在中国兴办邮政事业，先机必然源自上乘的邮票，当仁不让，此优良邮票必由我司之先进工艺印制。

为您效劳荣幸之至

W.W. 德纳罗

谨上

---

1 德纳罗公司一管之见。
2 即 6 月 8 日德纳罗致金登干函。

敬呈：金登干先生

斯托里门，西南区

1877 年 7 月 6 日金登干致德纳罗函

No. 2483

大清帝国海关

总税务司署伦敦办事处

斯托里门 8 号，圣詹姆斯公园，西南区

1877 年 7 月 6 日

阁下：

　　谨此确认收悉昨日来函，十分感谢您对本月 2 日邮政订货单之书面回复。

　　我完全同意您的看法，在运往中国途中，涂胶纸张会受潮破损，因此，我会询问如果将所需物料寄出，可否在那里刷胶。

　　昨日我已致函 W.W. 德纳罗先生，盼复，考虑到订货单是在中国准备的，希望他可以提出切实之建议，使得上海的海关造册处可在今年 10 月 1 日开工印制邮票。

金登干

谨上

致：德纳罗先生及公司

　　布伦希尔街

　　中东区

1877年7月6日德纳罗致金登干函

1877 年 7 月 6 日

阁下：

非常感谢您昨日的来信，以及所附的电报副本。我从信中知悉，您打算等电报有了答复再推动此事，此举甚为妥当。待您与中方进一步沟通之后，我再与您面晤此事。因为尽管各方反对，若总税务司执意在中国印制邮票，想必事出有因。届时，我司必竭尽所能，助您一臂之力。诚然，希望总税务司能交由我们率先承办印制业务。

想必您已收到了我们昨天的正式信函。

您非常友善的

W.W. 德纳罗

（请阅后页）

敬呈金登干先生

又及，刚刚收悉您今晨来信，倘若已拍板在中国印制邮票，那么试生产可以发往中国的合成胶之事，我司乐意之至。但是纸张在运往中国之前须加好外包装。

如我前述，如果最终决定在中国印制邮票，我司必竭尽所能助您一臂，但也希望总税务司能做出明智选择。当然，眼下只能静候中方复电，抑或您认为有哪些需要准备之事，比如印模和印版？

依您信中所示，将订购单所附图表奉还。

1877 年 12 月 17 日金登干致德纳罗函 [1]

订单号：193

大清帝国海关

总税务司署伦敦办事处

斯托里门 8 号，圣詹姆斯公园，西南区

1877 年 12 月 17 日

阁下：

贵方应尽快向本办事处提交附表（一式两份）的投标书（投标书一式两份），征购品项详列其中。

如不愿意签订合约，请尽快将表格（一式两份）归还本处。

金登干 主任

谨上

致：德纳罗先生及公司

布伦希尔街

中东区

1　德纳罗公司 1877 年 12 月 18 日收到。

1877 年 12 月 19 日德纳罗标书

大清帝国海关

订单号：193　　　　　　　江海关[1]　　　　　申请编号：19

副本

书籍装帧用硬布封面的投标

我们谨此提供最佳质量及制作的物品（以买方核查为准），从订货日期起，七周之内，在伦敦船上交货，物品在下表中详细说明，每件物品单独报价，加在一起净现金总价 56 英镑 3 先令 4 便士。

签名：德纳罗公司

地址：伦敦中东区布伦希尔街 110 号

日期：1877 年 12 月 19 日

物品详细描述：

1000 份深绿色硬布封面，大小需能包装 37 张淡色用纸（折成 4 开），样本附后。封皮带有镀金标记，扉页标题的汉字摹本附后，反面印刷字母。

1　上海海关的旧名。

《圣谕广训》[1]

帛黎[2]

江海关

造册处（法语）

帝国海关（法语）

备注：正反两边都有漂亮的暗压花纹，正面的汉字烫金，背面同样烫金和暗压花纹。

两边的边缘上都要印上一些整洁合适的设计。

注：这些封面希望能尽早运抵中国。

数量：1000

金额：54 英镑 3 先令 4 便士

物品总价：54 英镑 3 先令 4 便士

以最好方式装运的包装费：2 英镑

从装运代理人处收到提单后支付的净额：56 英镑 3 先令 4 便士

---

1 雍正二年（1724）出版的官修典籍，训谕世人守法和应有的德行、道理。

2 A. Théophile Piry，法国人，时任同文馆法文教习，1911 年就任邮政总办。1918 年 7 月 10 日在法国病逝。

1877 年 12 月 21 日订货函 [1]

订单号 : 193

大清帝国海关

总税务司署伦敦办事处

斯托里门 8 号，圣詹姆斯公园，西南区

1877 年 12 月 17 日

阁下 :

务请按照本月 19 日标书要求提供 1000 份深绿色硬布封面。

如您收悉此信，敬请告知何时能查验货品，我将不胜感激。

主任代表 F.E. 泰勒 [2]

谨上

请呈 : 德纳罗先生及公司

布伦希尔街 110 号

中东区

---

1 信函使用"大清帝国海关总税务司署伦敦办事处 / 西南区圣詹姆斯公园斯托里门 8 号"公函纸。

2 艾尔兰在《大龙邮票》一书中曾说 F.E. 泰勒是金登干的一位朋友，从德纳罗档案保存的文件来看，泰勒与金登干均为伦敦办事处的雇员，金登干不在时，行使主任职权。

1877 年 12 月 22 日德纳罗致金登干函

1877 年 12 月 22 日

阁下：

您昨日来函说已接受我司本月 19 日之投标，货品为 1000 份深绿色硬布封面，甚为感谢。此订单我司将立即着手处理。

您要求寄回我司投标函副本，我司表示理解，但由于误认为您所给的副本是供我们使用的，故已将其装订于案卷之中。有鉴于此，烦请您再寄一张表格，将不胜感激，会及时填写并奉回。

为您效劳荣幸之至
W.W. 德纳罗
谨上

呈：金登干先生

斯托里门 8 号

圣詹姆斯公园

1877 年 12 月 24 日函 [1]

备　忘

索引号：3176　　　　　　　　　　　　　1877 年 12 月 24 日

（回复时引用）

自：主任　　　　　　　　　　　　　致：德纳罗先生及公司

大清帝国海关伦敦办事处

斯托里门 8 号，圣詹姆斯公园，西南区

根据您的要求，随函附上一份标书副本，请您签字并寄回。

1　此函写在伦敦办事处的格式便笺上，销盖德纳罗公司"1877 年 12 月 27 日收到 /
登记"戳。

1878 年 1 月 22 日海关伦敦办事处函 [1]

大清帝国海关伦敦办事处

斯托里门 8 号，圣詹姆斯公园，西南区

1878 年 1 月 22 日

订单号：193

硬布封面事宜

阁下：

1. 刷唛要求

关于贵司 193 号订单的货品，请在包装箱等物品上，依照随函所附的说明刷唛，编号从 1 开始。

2. 装运清单一式两份

装运须知将寄送贵司，随后寄回我处，请妥善填写所附装运清单，一式两份，需写明每个箱子或包裹的编号、简介、重量、尺寸和价值等，以便船运和投保。

3. 装运账单一式三份

装运账单也需尽快返回，所附的装箱明细，填写一式两份，写明每个箱子的内装物品明细。另，提供货款发票一式三份，所到货

1　此函为伦敦办事处的格式文件。

品顺序须与标书一致。买方在收到船运代理人的提货单后会即刻安排付款。

金登干 主任

谨上

呈：德纳罗先生及公司

　　布伦希尔街 110 号，中东区

（登入出口日记账 A 卷）[1]

1　此句为德纳罗公司归档时所书注。

海关伦敦办事处物品刷唛方法 [1]

中国海关总税务司署伦敦办事处

刷唛方法

　　装箱唛头须与本图例所示一致，每件物品的顶部均要刷注大清帝国海关的专用印记 ☯ ，目的地标注在前面，所装物品的唛头通常刷在左侧，以便中方遵奉。

　　桶状、片状以及袋装物品，都应尽可能依循上述方法，如果物品确实难以刷唛，应牢固地拴上标签，如下图的线圈所示，标签内容同上。

　　标签应拴在线圈内侧，以保护地址不受磨损。

1　此件为印刷品，应为海关伦敦办事处采购物品的通行包装标记方法。

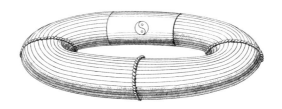

注：大清海关印记的构图是一个圆绕着两个相等的半圆 ⌇ ，

即：◉ 右侧的图形是黑色的，上半圆的中心或圆眼为白色，而左

侧的半圆是白色的，圆眼为黑色。

档案英文

1877 年 5 月 1 日中国海关的询函

May 1st 77

1. What would - say - one million postage stamps made in England cost? (£50 to £60)

2. What would it cost to procure machinery, plant and paper to make in China say one million stamps per week? (Hypothetically)

3. What would be the cost per month of the English personnel required for producing one million stamps a week, taking into consideration that all elementary manual labour can be had here. (Will write full report)[1]

Yellow	Imperial colour
Red & Pink	Happy
Blue	Mourning
Green	Happy
Brown	Mourning

---

1 三个问题后括号内文字及下面五种颜色的表述均为铅笔书写。

1877 年 5 月 22 日金登干致德纳罗函

London Office of the Inspectorate General of
Chinese Imperial Maritime Customs:
8, Storey's Gate, St. James's Park, S.W.
22 May 1877

Dear Sir,

I enclose two sketches I received from Peking some time ago.

In the Ying & Yang device , the dark side should be upper-most . I also sent you a sketch of the Dragon on a large scale.

I shall be glad if you will let me have your report before next mail day (Friday) as I telegraphed to China that details would be ready last Friday.

Yours truly,

J.D. Campbell

P.S.

Will you kindly return the two small sketches, when you have done with them.

J.D.C.

1877 年 5 月 23 日金登干致德纳罗函

8, Storey's Gate, St. James's Park, S.W.

23 May 77

My dear Sir,

In each of the two small sketches I sent you yesterday, there is a globe, floating in space, which is intended for the "Yin & Yang".

Yours truly

J.D. Campbell

1877年6月8日备忘录

June 8th 1877

Memo

In my second interview with Mr. Campbell on May 3rd, I explained to him that we only do business with English houses, and that we should, therefore, hesitate to supply the Chinese Government direct. He, however, told me that the Oriental Bank would be prepared upon the occasion of each order which might reach us through him to vouch for the payment of the amount entailed.

W.W.D.

1877 年 6 月 8 日德纳罗致金登干函

Confidential

110 Bunhill Row,
London, E.C.,
June 8th 1877[1]

Sir,

We have before us, together with your telegraphic[2] answers thereto, the memorandum[3] which you recently received from the Inspector General of Chinese Maritime Customs; and in fulfilment of our promise we will now, with your permission, proceed to give you such information as may be requisite to enable you to furnish a Report upon the subject of Adhesive Stamps to that gentleman.

We will in this letter chiefly confine ourselves to stamps which are used for the Postage Service, seeing that it is they with which you are immediately concerned, but we will, with your permission, before closing also give such particulars about Revenue, Customs or Law Stamps as will show the conditions which they have to fulfil.

Adhesive stamps are produced upon four different systems, viz.,

（A）By the intaglio printing process.

（B）By the lithographic printing process.

1　此日期档案中用铅笔删去，并在边上注明 "Mr. Campbell altered this date to the 18th. See his letter of June 29 1877"，后亦删去。

2　"telegraphic" 一词系中铅笔添加。

3　"memorandum" 系将 "telegram" 用铅笔修改。

（C）By the embossing process, that being generally combined with one or other of the printing processes.

（D）By the surface-printing process.

We will deal with these processes in the order in which they are given, but before entering into the matter we should explain that the various specimens of stamps to which we shall refer as being given in our appendices, have advisedly been overprinted with the word "Cancelled" in order to destroy them.

（A）In the intaglio printing process, the configuration of the stamp is recessed into a steel die by means of a knife-like instrument termed a "graver". Supposing for example, it were wished to print the letter A by the process in question, the lines requisite to form that letter would have to be cut or scratched into a steel die to a depth which would be about equal to the thickness of the paper on which we write. In order to print the letter from such a die, printing ink, consisting of boiled linseed oil mixed with any colored pigment which might be required (e.g. blue, red, green, yellow, &c., &e.) would have to be rubbed over the die with a piece of rag, the effect being that the whole surface of the die would be smeared over with the printing ink, and that it would lodge itself in the recesses form- ing the letter A, so that when in the next operation a clean piece of rag were taken and rubbed to and fro over the surface of the die, so as to remove the printing ink from it, that which had lodged in the recesses would not be disturbed. We should then have a die with a perfectly clean surface, but with the incised letter A filled with printing ink, and it is obvious that if by any means we could so arrange as to convey the printing ink from the recesses in the die to the surface of a piece of paper, we should have a printed letter A. This result is effected by laying a piece of paper upon the die, and passing the two together between rollers which are so contrived as to press the paper with considerable force against the die. As the printing ink has a greater affinity or kindness for the paper than for the metal, so soon as the paper is pressed sufficiently close to the die to bring the surface of the former in contact with the ink which is in the recesses of the latter the ink clings to the paper and accompanies it when removed from the die, rather than remain in its recesses. Such is an outline of the method of intaglio printing, and it will be readily understood that the same explanation would apply whether the form of the print were merely that of a simple letter A or whether it were of an elaborate character, like the intaglio printed stamps at the top of our Appendix A, each line of which represents a recess in the plate.

The stamps are not, of course, printed singly, but in considerable numbers. In this country, there are generally as many as 240 stamps to a sheet, seeing that there are 240 units of our currency (i.e. pence)in the pound; besides which a sheet containing 240 Postage Stamps is a very convenient size to manufacture. It should be understood that the 240 stamps which are printed on a sheet are not obtained by taking 240 separate impressions upon different parts of the sheet from a printing die or plate containing only one stamp, but from a printing plate containing as many repeats of the stamps as have to appear in the printed sheet. Nevertheless, the engraver has only to cut or engrave one stamp. The small plate or die on which he does so is termed the original and becomes the parent of the full sized plates used to print from, and which, as before stated, generally contain 240 multiples of the stamp. These working plates are obtained from the original die by means of an apparatus, which it would be difficult to describe without diagrams. Suffice it to say that a soft steel roller is passed under great pressure to and fro over the original die until the metal of the roller has been squeezed into the recesses of the die, the effect being that exact counterparts of the recesses in the die are formed in relief upon the roller. After such a roller had been hardened by being plunged at a red heat into cold water, it would if rolled with pressure over a metallic plate furnish a facsimile of the original die, seeing that the projections in the roller would make corresponding depressions in the plate under treatment. Not only may one impression be taken from the roller in this manner, but any number may be obtained by repeating the like process, so long as the roller remains in good condition, and of its deterioration there is not much fear, seeing that it is brought to a great hardness before being used. But even if it should wear out, nothing more would be necessary than to revert to the original die in order to obtain a near roller. Consequently, we have the means of making any number of facsimiles of the original die; and by the aid of certain appliances we are enabled to make these in plates of metal at equal distances apart so as to form working plates of 240 or any less number of multiples.

（B）For the lithographic printing process, the original die is prepared in exactly the same manner as in that for intaglio printing; but instead of its being multiplied in order to form working plates in the manner above described, prints are taken from it upon "transfer paper". This consists of ordinary paper dressed with a preparation of starch so as to form a soluble film upon its surface. The print is taken on this film, and whilst still wet it is laid face downwards upon a polished slab of lithographic stone. This kind of stone has an affinity for a greasy substance like printing ink, and when the print is laid on it the stone is well disposed towards the ink to which it is thus introduced. As, however, the object is not only to bring the print into contact with the stone, but actually to transfer it from the paper to the stone, the paper is slightly damped at the back, so that the soluble film which is on its surface may be acted upon by the water. So soon as the paper has been sufficiently moistened, it is forcibly pressed against the stone by passing it under a special form of press. The consequence of this operation is that the print is brought into very close contact with the stone, whilst the soluble film having been disengaged from the paper, and having consequently thrown off the ink there from, the latter clings to the stone as a matter of necessity. We have thus a somewhat porous stone with a printed impression upon its surface, which, being oleaginous, will resist water, at the same time having an affinity for printing ink, that being of a greasy nature. If, therefore, a sponge charged with water be passed over the stone, those parts thereof which are unprinted will absorb moisture, whilst the printed parts will throw off or resist the water. Consequently, if a roller charged with printing ink (composed of boiled linseed oil and pigment) be passed over the stone so moistened, the printing ink will adhere to the greasy pattern upon the stone, but will not adhere to the bare portion thereof by reason of the moisture thereon. We should have explained that before the stone is actually printed from, the transferred pattern is fixed thereto by the application of an acid solution which has the effect of selling the pattern firmly to the stone, so that it may be printed from without injury. When a layer of printing ink has been imparted to the pattern in the manner described, all that is necessary to obtain a printed impression is to lay a sheet of paper upon the stone and to pass it through the press. By this means, the paper is brought into close contact with the face of the stone, and the printing ink which has been spread over the pattern by means of the roller is pressed on to the paper, so that when the sheet is lifted from the stone it is found to be printed with the desired pattern. By way of illustration we give on Appendix A a specimen of a stamp printed by the process under consideration.

It will be understood that 240 or any other number of stamps can be obtained on a sheet by merely taking the requisite number of single prints on transfer paper from the original die, and laying them down at the proper distance from one another upon the stone before the back of the transfer paper is damped as above described. Thus, any number of stamps can be transferred to a stone in like manner as the single one we have considered.

(C) As we have already stated, the embossing process of producing postage stamps is generally combined with one or other of the printing processes. As, however, we are dealing with the printing processes separately we will not here consider their application to embossed stamps, seeing that it will be sufficient to describe the manner in which the embossment is made, since when once the printing processes are understood it is only necessary to conceive that one or other of them has been resorted to before embossing a stamp to understand clearly the manner in which it has been produced. As will be seen by the specimens of embossed stamps in Appendix A, it is usual to confine the embossment to the central figure of the stamp, leaving the rest of the configuration to be carried out by printing; nevertheless, there would be no difficulty in extending the area of embossment were it so desired. The process is as follows: A soft steel block or die is taken and the head or other device to be embossed is scooped out of it by means of hardened steel tools. So soon as the pattern has been completed, the die is hardened, in the manner described in connection with the first process, and impressions are taken from it in square leaden blocks of the size of a stamp. By means of a fly-press, there being a special contrivance to keep the blocks exactly square, even when they are subjected to such a pressure as is requisite to make the lead flow into the recesses of the steel die, so as to form a perfect counterpart thereof. 240 of such leads, or a number corresponding to the multiples required in the working plate, are struck with the die, and they are then grouped together with accuracy so as to form an exact counterpart of the plate which is required, excepting that those parts which will be sunken in the plate project in the leads. The leads thus arranged are placed in the trough of a battery so that a copper counterpart of them may be produced by the electrotyping process. This copper counterpart when removed from the leads constitutes the working plate, and in fact contains as many exact duplicates of the original die as there were leads. After it has been mounted by being screwed down to a plate of iron, it is put under a powerful fly-press, having a thick sheet of warm gutta percha laid on the top of it; the press is now put in action, by which repeated blows are applied to the gutta percha, so as to drive it into the recesses of the plate. When the gutta percha has thus been forced into every recess of the plate, the former is lifted off the latter and fastened coincidently with the plate to the upper slab of the fly-press. The sheet of stamps to be embossed, having already been printed, is then laid face downwards upon the plate and visited with a heavy blow from the press, the gutta percha counterpart coming down with the upper slab thereof and forcing the paper into every recess of the plate. Thus, when it is removed from the plate and turned face upwards, those parts which were driven into the recesses of the plate are found to be raised or embossed to a height proportionate to the depth of the recesses which they occupied.

Now each of these three processes for the production of stamps is open to very grave objection, not only because they lack refinement, and consequently produce but comparatively clumsy work, but what is of more importance the stamps produced thereby can not only be forged but can be cleaned from a printed obliteration, and so fraudulently used a second time. It will be understood from what has gone before that in printing upon the intaglio system the printing ink is left in ridges upon the paper. These ridges are very apparent when the ink is wet, and although they are much reduced in height by the shrinking of the ink in the process of drying, it is evident (although the difference can hardly be detected by the naked eye) that the stamp must remain thicker in the printed portions than in the plain, seeing that the whole of the ink which filled the recesses in the plate passed to the paper in the form of ridges. This condition offers very great facility to the forger, for its existence renders it possible to produce absolute facsimiles of the printing plate in the following manner. A certain preparation of wax and asphaltum, called etch-ing-ground, is applied to the surface of a steel or copper plate in a thin layer and allowed to set hard. The intaglio printed stamp to be dealt with is then laid face downwards upon the prepared side of the plate and the two together are passed through a pair of pressure rollers, the effect being that the ridges of the print press into the etching-ground, and by reason of its brittleness break it up. The plate is then treated with acid, which attacks these portions that have been exposed through the fractures of the etching-ground, whilst where this has been left intact, or in other words in those parts where no ridges of print have fallen, the metal is protected from the action of the acid. The ridges of an intaglio plate may in fact be considered as almost equivalent to knife-edges cutting through the protecting mantle which is put upon the plate, thereby exposing it in those parts where they fall to the action of the acid. Thus although the ridges cannot be brought actually to indent the metallic plate, it is possible through their agency to obtain in an indirect manner counterparts of the ridges, or in other words to reproduce the original plate from which they were printed; the depth of the indentations in the forged plate depending of course upon the length of time during which the action of the acid may be maintained. As we have shown you, we have in this manner produced copies of intaglio stamp printing plates, so exact that it is impossible to distinguish the forged stamps printed with them from the true ones.

This particular mode of forgery is applicable only to intaglio printed stamps, for in them alone is the pattern produced in ridges of printing ink, seeing that both in the lithographic process and the surface printing process, which we will presently describe, the ink is merely laid on the paper superficially, that is to say in so thin a layer that it rises to no appreciable height. The lithographic process is, however, very unsuitable for stamp printing, the prints being unavoidably ill-defined or blurred instead of being sharp and distinct——so essential for real security——besides which stamps printed by that process, as well as those printed by the intaglio process, are exposed to forgery by a method very much simpler than that above described. The success of the transfer processes of forgery depends upon certain properties possessed by the drying oils, one of which (linseed oil)is of necessity used for printing ink. Although after exposure to the air printing ink becomes hard, still be it ever so dry it only has to be soaked in a dilute solution of hydrochloric acid to make it assume almost its original viscid condition. If a dry print be taken, and be subjected to such treatment, it is brought to very much the same condition as when first printed, and if it be laid on a lithographic stone and passed through a press, a portion of the softened ink will adhere to the stone, sufficient to enable a skilful operator by careful manipulation to bring the pattern thus made upon the stone into a fit condition to print from. That is the ordinary process of forgery by transfer, but a very much more refined one is available, by which very faithful copies of intaglio or lithographic printed stamps can be obtained, seeing that with a good pattern upon the stone the lithographer is capable of producing impressions which would well pass for intaglio prints, and he can of course with a proper pattern upon the stone copy stamps produced originally by his branch of the printing art. In the process we allude to instead of depending upon the peculiar behaviour of the printing ink when subjected to the action of dilute hydrochloric acid, the affinity which the printing ink has for an oleaginous substance is turned to account. The stamp to be operated upon is immersed in a cup of water and left to soak until the water has penetrated the substance of the paper, when it sinks to the bottom of the cup. A little oil is then floated upon the surface of the water and the stamp is by means of a pair of tweezers brought in a diagonal direction face upwards through the layer of oil, the action being that while the wet paper repels the oil, the kindly printing ink upon its surface receives a layer thereof. As a consequence, the plain portions of the stamp are left perfectly clean, whilst the printed portion has a layer of oil on its surface, which can be readily transferred to a lithographic stone, so that a very perfect pattern from which to print is obtained, seeing that the oil has sufficient affinity for the stone to cling to it readily.

With the embossing process, the forger would have if anything even less difficulty than with the intaglio or lithographic printing process. This plan of operation would be to support a stamp underneath with plaster of Paris, or some other suitable material, and then to take a cast from it as a first step to a copy in metal. This could easily be obtained by the electrotype process, or indeed by a variety of methods, and it would yield any number of paper impressions which might be required.

In addition to these inherent defects in the processes which have been under review, there are two other good reasons against their employment, the first being that they do not afford the means of printing the stamps in "fugitive" ink; and the second that the stamps produced by them are, independently of their liability to be forged, but imperfect productions. The consideration of the first mentioned defect, we will postpone for the present; at the same time, we should point out that the intaglio printed stamps are not only clumsy in appearance, but that they are neither so clear nor so serviceable as they should be, seeing that the ink lying in ridges is likely to smudge with abrasion, which of necessity must frequently happen in the handling of Postage Stamps, no less than in their transit through the post. The lithographic stamps, as we have before stated, are altogether inferior in quality, whilst the embossed stamps are not only somewhat crude in themselves, but are very bulky in comparison with the others on account of the embossment, besides which they are liable to be flattened by pressure.

（D）Now all these considerations have led us to discard the three processes which we have discussed above in favour of the improved surface stamp printing process which we succeeded in perfecting some thirty years ago, and which is illustrated by the last group of specimens on Appendix A. This process is in fact now employed for almost all the stamps which we manufacture, and it enables us to produce stamps which are secure against forgery and are proof against being fraudulently cleaned and used a second time. It may almost be described as being the reverse of the intaglio process, seeing that instead of the pattern being cut or recessed in the original die, the die is so cut as to leave the pattern in relief. The printing or working plates are made from this relief die very much in the same manner as the embossing working plates as described above, excepting, of course, that the final result is to obtain a working plate with the pattern projected instead of being recessed. The process of printing consists in passing a special kind of roller charged with "fugitive" printing ink over the working plate, so that those parts with which it comes in contact (i.e. the raised patterns) are charged with a mere superficies of ink. When a sheet of paper is laid upon this inked plate and is subjected to pressure (and the pressure is enormous, being produced by a special kind of press) the ink is transferred from the plate to the paper, by which means an exquisitely fine print is produced, seeing that great delicacy can be obtained in the original die, and as a consequence in the working plate, whilst a perfect impression of this plate can be made on the paper, and that too in such a manner that the pattern is in the same plane as the paper, not in ridges as in the case of the intaglio printed stamps. Consequently, the surface printed stamps are not only refined in appearance (a matter of the first moment), but they are secure against the process of forgery which depends for success upon the pattern being raised above the surface of the paper. The great importance of having stamps of a very refined character must be at once apparent by the reflection that the more perfect their nature, the more able are they to defy imitation by drawing, engraving, or any other such process, for were they not productions of a high character, and indeed of their kind as perfect as are to be obtained, a facility for their imitation would offer itself to a skillful operator, even were it not in his power to employ the stamps themselves in any way as auxiliaries by either of the methods of forgery discussed previously.

We have now arrived at that point at which it will be useful to show the conditions which our fugitive inks have to fulfil. The inks in question are termed fugitive because they retreat or disappear under the attacks of solvents such as could be used to remove from a stamp a printed obliteration, that is to say they are soluble in the hydrocarbons and similar liquids. The intaglio and lithographic printing processes do not admit of the use of such inks, and as a consequence stamps printed by either of those processes are unaffected by the liquids above referred to, and in fact they may when once dry be soaked in benzine (we take benzine as the most convenient of the solvents which could be used to clean stamps) for an indefinite period without any appreciable result. Postage stamps are cancelled by the impress of an obliterating mark with a hand-stamp, such a mark as is shown at the top of our Appendix B. The ink employed for that purpose is of a peculiar description termed "endorsing" ink, and when dry it has the property of being nearly insoluble in benzine. If, then, a stamp, printed in "fugitive" ink be obliterated with the endorsing ink, the obliteration cannot be removed without destroying the stamp, as will be seen by referring to Appendix B. The second example is a $3^{d.}$ English Postage Stamp obliterated with "endorsing" ink and so left; the following one a stamp similarly obliterated, but subsequently treated with benzine. As will be seen the effect has been to destroy the stamp, whilst the obliteration is but little disturbed. Consequently, if stamps printed in such fugitive ink be efficiently cancelled by a printed obliteration, they cannot be cleansed for fraudulent use a second time, as they could be were the ink not of a fugitive character, as is exemplified by the intaglio printed stamps in Appendix B. These two stamps being printed in ordinary printing ink, the obliteration in the lower one has been almost entirely washed away, whilst the stamp has been left undisturbed. It will be understood that before it was treated with benzine, the lower example had exactly the same appearance as the upper one. It is, then, of the utmost importance that Postage Stamps should be printed in fugitive ink, so that the obliteration may be an efficient agent of destruction.

As we have before stated, this obliteration is usually imparted by means of a hand-stamp, but where large quantities of letters have to be dealt with, an obliterating machine supplied by us is used for the purpose, similar to that shown in the photograph at the top of Appendix C. This machine (worked by hand) is comparatively cheap, its cost being only £12 (exclusive of packing etc.) and is capable of obliterating a very great number of stamps in the course of a day. It is fitted with a stamp or a pair of stamps, as illustrated by the photographs in Appendices C & D. One of these serves to obliterate the stamp with a secret symbol or combination of letters showing the office at which the obliteration took place, whilst the other being placed in the machine alongside its companion is impressed upon the body of the envelope and gives the name of the town at which the obliteration took place as well as the time and date thereof. The latter stamp cannot be considered as serving the purpose of an obliterating mark, but rather as a companion to the true obliterating mark. It, however, gives in one sense the most important part of the obliteration, viz. the date. In order to achieve this object the body of the stamp is perforated with four slots into which are fitted steel type, of which the small one uppermost bears an initial letter indicating the hour, whilst the other three serve to indicate respectively the day, month, and the year. The head of the stamp unscrews in such a manner as to afford ready access to the above-referred-to slots, so that the type may be changed as often as is requisite. The combination of the two stamps, i.e. the true obliterating stamp and its companion having been devised for a special purpose in England, it is questionable whether the same arrangement would be serviceable elsewhere. We are inclined to think that it would be better to employ but one stamp containing the name of the cancelling station and the date, as is shown in our sketch at the foot of Appendix D.

When the stamps are not used in the machine, they are fitted into a handle, as shown in the photographs above referred to. This handle, as will be seen, is provided with three holes in its head. The central hole is employed when only one stamp is used, as occasionally happens; the two outer ones are employed when two stamps are used in conjunction.

Reverting to the consideration of the ink, we should state that although the primary object of using fugitive ink is to render stamps secure against being used more than once, another most important advantage is gained by the use of such ink, viz. the impossibility of reproducing stamps printed therewith by the transfer process, a method particularly applicable, as we have shown, to stamps produced by the other systems. The success of the transfer process of forgery demands that the stamp to be copied should be printed in an oleaginous ink, and since the fugitive ink is not oleaginous it sets that process at defiance, for the fugitive ink is not subject to swell and become viscid when steeped in dilute hydrochloric acid, nor will it receive oil when applied to it in the manner we have described in connection with stamps printed by the other methods. Our fugitive ink, in short, being entirely free from those properties which render ordinary printing ink so unfit for stamp printing, it follows that stamps printed therewith by the most perfect system (i.e. the surface) are undoubtedly as secure against forgery as it is possible to render them, more especially as independently of the impossibility of transferring them in the manner we have discussed, the lithographic process is not sufficiently refined to yield prints that would in any way compare with surface printed stamps.

So far we have made reference exclusively to Postage Stamps. We will now, however, as briefly as possible explain the conditions which have to be fulfilled by Revenue, Customs, and Law Stamps. In the case of the former, the obliteration is always made by the Post Office officials, and it is, therefore, possible to enforce the use of a hand-stamp such as we have described, but with stamps which have to be used upon various documents, the case is different, as the duty of cancelling the stamp usually devolves upon the user thereof, and it would be unreasonable to expect that every individual called upon to affix a stamp to a document should be required to provide himself with a proper cancelling mark. Such stamps must almost of necessity, therefore, be cancelled by the simple process of writing across them. The ink in which they are printed has, consequently, to fulfil a totally different function to that in which the Postage Stamps are printed, which is fugitive only under the treatment of such liquids as could be employed for the removal of a printed cancellation; whereas in the case of the Revenue and like Stamps it is imperative to employ an ink which would be fugitive to such reagents as could be used for removing a written cancellation. Nevertheless, although such stamps are as a rule cancelled by writing, it is in some cases a matter of convenience to cancel them by a printed obliteration (in the Law Courts, for instance, where hand-stamps are always within reach). Consequently, in order to be fully protective, the ink in which such stamps are printed must be not only fugitive to reagents calculated to remove a written cancellation, but also to such as would remove a printed cancellation. This necessity has brought into use what we term "doubly fugitive" inks, such as we employ in the printing of Revenue, Customs and Law Stamps. We only have three "doubly fugitive" inks, specimens of which are given upon Appendix E. The doubly fugitive light purple ink in which are printed the stamps at the head of this Appendix is generally employed for the lower duties of stamps, whilst the higher duties are by way of distinction printed in the green and the darker purple, like those in the specimens which follow. All three colours are, as we have said, "doubly fugitive", as will be seen by referring to our Appendix above referred to, wherein by the side of an uncancelled stamp we give in each case two specimens of cancelled stamps, one obliterated by writing and the other by printing. We have in each case treated that obliterated by writing with oxalic acid and that obliterated by printing with benzene. As will be seen, the former treatment destroys beyond restoration the colour of the stamp, whilst the latter treatment washes the body of the stamp away. In each case, the obliteration is much less disturbed than the stamp which it covers. Now, the Revenue, Customs and Law Stamps differ from the Postage Stamps only in this, that the former three are printed in our "doubly fugitive" inks, whilst the latter are printed in our "singly fugitive" inks. The conditions of security and of manufacture for both kinds of stamps are precisely the same, excepting that the former kinds are more difficult to print than the latter. This remark applies especially to the green and dark purple, as they are produced by a peculiar process which renders them exceedingly sensitive——so much so as to preclude their use where there is any chance of their being exposed to moisture or rough treatment of any kind, seeing that they are immediately destroyed by the action of water or by abrasion. When, therefore, Revenue, Customs, or Law Stamps are exposed to wear, the only colour available is the light purple in which are printed the stamps given at the head of our Appendix E. This colour, whilst possessing the peculiar "doubly fugitive" properties we have described, is as firm as the "singly fugitive" inks in which the Postage Stamps are printed.

Whilst we are upon subject of Revenue Stamps, it is well to call attention to a peculiar form of such stamps which is employed by the Government of India. They find it expedient in the case of most legal instruments to enforce the use of most legal instruments to enforce the use of what are termed "Stamped Papers" consisting of sheets of watermarked paper with elaborate stamps printed at their heads. Providing the instrument runs into more space than the "Stamped Paper" affords, it is continued upon ordinary paper cut down to the size of the "Stamped Paper", which forms its commencing page. Such "Stamped Papers" are to be highly recommended on account of the security which they afford. We give a specimen of one of the duties upon Appendix L, but in the case of India there are more than 100 duties, all of which are distinctive in device.

Having discussed in outline the various conditions and processes of adhesive stamp manufacture, it becomes important to show how the particular process in vogue is carried out, and what precautions are taken by the Governmental authorities in regard to control. We will, therefore, proceed to describe the course through which a ream of stamps (-500 sheets) would go in its production.

The paper which is used contains a special watermark for each description of stamp, such watermark not only affording an additional protection as presenting an initial obstacle to the forger, but serving for purposes of control, seeing that stamps must be printed only upon the paper specially designed for them. The example at the top of Appendix F is a piece of watermarked stamp paper just as it came from the paper-making machine, being, however, only one of many descriptions of paper which we make for different kinds of stamps, the watermark varying in each description. The Dandyrolls (the special apparatus employed in the production of the watermarks in the paper) are kept in a locked-up strong-room by Government officials, and are taken out by them only when a supply is required of the particular kind of paper for which a roll is applicable. An officer remains by the paper-making machine during the whole time that the paper is being made, and returns the dandyroll to the strong-room so soon as it is done with. We should mention that two officers are constantly employed in controlling the manufacture of our stamps papers, and that they keep the stock under lock and key. Of this they serve out such quantities as may be required from time to time, counting it carefully sheet by sheet before parting with it. Each delivery which they make is recorded in an Account Book. Before the paper is handed over to us it undergoes another process of counting, and after we have satisfied ourselves by a third count that it is correct in quantity, we hand a receipt to the authorities for it, and pass it through the processes necessary to prepare it for stamp printing. Amongst them is the gumming process, by which a quantity of gum is applied to the back of the sheet sufficient to secure the adhesion of the stamps to letters &c. The lower example in Appendix F was cut from the same piece of paper as the upper one, and after being subjected to the process above referred to was highly glazed. The paper having been brought into this condition is taken to the printing department, over which Government officers preside. Before being received there, it is carefully counted in order to make sure that the right number of sheets are taken into the room and an account of it is recorded in the proper book. The printing process is carried on under the immediate control of Government Officers, who have in fact the entire charge of the room, no less than the apparatus employed therein, the principal part of which, such as the plates and dies they deposit in strong rooms (fire and thief-proof) for safety during the night as well as for Sundays and holidays. The fact of there being no fewer than 40 Government Officers in our establishment superintending such work, and that the aggregate representative value of the Stamps which we produce annually, amounts to many million pounds will speak for itself as to the rigid system of control which prevails here, and will, we doubt not, ensure its appreciation.

We should explain that we carry on work for many Governments, each of which employs their own officers of control, so that we find it necessary to establish a separate printing department for each government. Supplying, as we do, the whole of the higher values of Stamps for the English Government, as well as the whole of those for that of India and the under mentioned countries, it will be readily understood that the manufacture of stamps by us is one of a most extensive character.

Countries for which we manufacture stamps

England	Antigua
India	Bahamas
Barbados	Nevis
Bermuda	St. Christopher
British Guiana	St. Helena
British Honduras	St. Lucia
Cope of Good Hope	Sierra Leone
Ceylon	Straits Settlements
Dominica	Tasmania
Gambia	Trinidad
Gold Coast	Virgin Islands

Hong Kong	West Australia
Jamaica	Orange Free States
Lagos	New South Wales
Malta	South Australia
Mauritius	New Zealand
Montserrat	Victoria
Natal	

and many other foreign governments[1]

As we have stated above, the different Governments for whom we work have each a separate and distinct staff of officers for the purpose of supervision; nevertheless, the system of control which is adopted in each of our manufacturing Departments is similar to that which we have described above, and, as previously stated, the officers in charge have full control over all the apparatus and material engaged in the work under their supervision, so that it becomes impossible for our workpeople, even if they were dishonestly disposed in any way to rob the Government whose work they are executing. The work is in fact us much under the control of the Governments concerned as if it were done in a Government office, we, however, being responsible for the proper conduct of the practical operations.

We will for the moment, with your permission, leave the subject of Adhesive Stamps to discuss a question which we think might be of interest to the Chinese Government, viz. that of Postage

---

1 此句英文系用铅笔添加。

Envelopes. As you are aware, we manufacture a large quantity of such envelopes for the English home Government, as well as for that of India. In the latter country, they are found to be of great service, not only to the general public, but also to the Post Office officials, whose business is greatly facilitated by the use of proper covers for letters, instead of the insecure covers which were much in use by the natives of India before they were supplied by the Government with Postage Envelopes. They possess also this advantage that being of a uniform size and character, they are much more easily dealt with than are letters covered by envelopes various as to size and shape. Circumstances may be different in China; nevertheless, we think that an appropriate form of Postage Envelope might be of great service there, seeing that even here in England it is found that the Postage Envelopes meet a real want, for to persons who are particular in such matters, an envelope with an embossed stamp has a better and neater appearance than one with an adhesive stamp affixed, to say nothing of the trouble saved (and that is the most important consideration) in affixing such stamps. In Appendix G, we give a specimen of one of the Postage Envelopes we make for the English Government, and in Appendix H a specimen of the two kinds or duties which we make for India. We reckon that the aggregate annual consumption of all these envelopes reaches no less than 58,000,000, a number which, moreover, is daily increasing. The Postage Stamp is embossed and printed with a coloured background in one operation, by a somewhat elaborate machine. The reason for the employment of the embossing process is that it is the only one which would give a really good result upon the envelopes at anything like a reasonable speed. True it is that the same objections apply to the stamps under discussion as those we pointed out in connection with embossed adhesive Postage Stamps; at the same time a certain protection is undoubtedly given to them by the fact of their being impressed upon envelopes which there would be some difficulty in copying. It would be difficult for a forger to match the exact quality of our paper, or, even if he should do so he would be puzzled to make a perfectly successful imitation of the envelopes. Hence, the envelope itself is in a measure secure from imitation; much more so when the stamp has been impressed upon it. As a fact, although the kind of stamps employed are not so secure as could be wished, we have never received any serious complaints as to our Postage Envelope being successfully imitated.

Now, we believe from what you have told us that the particular form of Envelope issued by the English and Indian Governments, as given in our Appendices G & H would not serve the requirements of the Chinese public, but that such an envelope as that in Appendix I would be more likely to be of service to them. More paper is wasted in cutting an envelope of this shape than in cutting one of the form of the English or Indian Postage Envelopes, but in other respects such an envelope would be almost as easily produced as they. The stamp could be affixed in the position we have indicated, or in any other place that might be desired. Underneath the envelopes in Appendix I, we have given drawings of two duties of embossed stamps which might be used upon them. It will be understood that the coloured parts represent the coloured background, whilst the white or shaded positions show those parts which would be raised in relief. We could produce such envelopes, of which we enclose 24, at about the rate of 11/. (eleven shillings) per thousand. This price would be exclusive of a charge of £65 (sixty five pounds) for the original embossing die and of £40 (forty pounds) for each duty die, but would include banding the envelopes in 24's with any printing on the band which might be required, packing them in tin-lined cases, and delivering them free on board ship in the London Docks.

It will of course be understood that we are in no way tied to the particular shape or size of our pattern envelope, but that we could at commensurate prices produce envelopes of any description that might be required both as to their form and the quality of paper employed besides being enabled to emboss them with stamps of any requisite device or duty.

Returning now to the Adhesive Postage Stamps, we beg to call your attention to our Appendix J, at the head of which you will find a design for what we should consider would be an appropriate watermark to employ in the paper for Chinese Stamps. This consists of the symbol Yin and Yang, deprived, however, of the nuclei, as those we could not render satisfactorily in the paper. Following the watermark design upon Appendix J, we give two sets or alternative designs for these different duties of Chinese Adhesive Postage Stamps. We have in each case adopted the same leading feature in the designs, that is to say the symbol Yin and Yang encircled by two dragons. Whilst, however, preserving this general characteristic, we have attempted to make the stamps as dissimilar as possible with the limited area at command, seeing that it is a matter of great importance that one value of stamp should be as strikingly unlike another as is practicable, not only to guard against the possibility of one duty being mistaken for another, but to render it impossible that by any manipulation a lower stamp should be converted into a higher one. For instance, supposing the 1 Candareen Stamp were the same in design and colour as the 2 Candareen stamp, the only difference between them being the Chinese characters denoting the duty, it is evident that the Chinese numeral 1 might be changed into a 2 and thus the 1 Candareen stamp be made to represent double its real value. That would be an instance of the simplest application of the particular mode of treatment in question, but it will be sufficient, we think, to show the desirability of making stamps unlike one another; and in fact experience has taught us that the more unlike they are in every way, the better. The designs which we have made are of the size of the English Postage Stamps, a size which it would be highly desirable to retain, seeing that all our apparatus is adapted for producing stamps of standard sizes (the one in question is the most appropriate for Postage Stamps) and that consequently any change as to size or shape would entail great expense.

The designs which we have been discussing are, of course, merely drawn by hand, and represent but very crudely the appearance which the finished stamps would present. We could throw a great amount of elaboration into the engraving of such designs, as will be at once apparent by referring to the specimen stamps given on Appendix A, or to the engraver's black proofs at the foot of Appendix J, from which it will be seen that we are enabled to bring our Stamps to a high degree of refinement, and that anything of the nature of an animal is capable of treatment quite as delicate as a head such as that adopted for the English stamps. The symbol Yin and Yang combined with the dragons would give considerable scope to our engravers; at the same time we think that the effect of the finished Stamps might be more pleasing were it possible to adopt some kind of animal for a centre-piece such as a tortoise, or any other creature typical of China. This, however, would be a matter entirely for the consideration of the Chinese authorities. It will be understood that the duties in the designs given upon Appendix J are merely suppositions, and that we should have no difficulty in changing them for any Chinese characters which might be required further, that our designs could easily be modified, and that we should be able to make a distinctive device for any number of duties which occasion might call for.

Supposing that we had to produce stamps after our designs, we should have to make an original master die bearing the symbol and the dragons; from that, we should make three other dies bearing the same symbol, and upon the one which we might select for the One Candareen duty to engrave the remainder of the work shown in the design. In like manner one of the other two dies would be completed for the two Candareen and the third for the five Candareen duty. If any additional dies were at any time required, the requisite number would be made from the master die, and the appropriate completing patterns engraved on them. By this system, we ensure the identity of the leading feature of each die or stamp (a great object as a matter of security), while we avoid the trouble and expense of engraving it upon each design, as would be the case did we not avail ourselves of a peculiar method, which we cannot attempt to describe in the compass of this letter, for reproducing the pattern in the original master die upon those intended to serve for the different duties.

So soon as the duty dies should have been completed in the manner described, they would furnish the means for producing the plates. One price for a master-die with the symbol of the dragons would be £75 (seventy five pounds); that for each duty die £50 (fifty pounds); and that for each printing plate of 240 multiples £85 (eighty five pounds); whilst the dandy roll required to produce the proposed watermark would cost £80 (eighty pounds). Our price for the stamps would be £54/3/4 (fifty four pounds three shillings and four pence)per million.[1] This price would include packing them in tin-lined cases and delivering them free on board ship in London. The price is for stamps gummed and perforated complete like the specimen quarter sheet of 12 Cents Hong Kong Postage Stamps given on Appendix K, and it is based upon the assumption that the stamps would be printed in sheets of 240 multiples, and that they would be subject to the like system of control as those we manufacture for the English, Indian or other Governments.

Regarding your request that we would give you some idea as to the cost of establishing Works in China for the production of Postage Stamps, we regret to say that it would be impossible for us

---

1　此段英文原档的左侧用铅笔标注 "Initial investment /Master die £75/Dandyroll £80/Total £155" 以及 "Special expense which would have to be entailed for each duty of stamps/Duty die £50/Printing plate £85/Total £135"。

to furnish even an approximate estimate of the expense which such a course would entail until we should know the probable number of stamps which would have to be produced per annum. At the same time, we may say that the cost of instituting such an establishment would be very heavy. Our feeling is, indeed, that it would be most unwise to attempt to carry out any such project until the Postage system had been given a fair trial, and until the production of the requisite stamps had been fully organized here in England; for even supposing that it were possible to establish Works in China competent to produce stamps of a satisfactory character, it is not for moment to be supplied that it would be possible in such Works to provide for new requirements, seeing that independently of any other consideration our long experience in such matters would be found to be almost indispensable (we say so in all modesty). Added to this, it would be impossible without an inordinate expense to establish and maintain such a staff in China as would be competent to carry out the initiatory work, for which our arrangements are so complete. The course we should recommend would be that in the event of the Chinese Government deciding to employ us for the production of their Postage Stamps, they should, in case the quantities required were at first small, solicit the assistance of the Home Government, or that of India, in the control of their Stamp manufacture. If they should think it desirable, we should, of course, be quite willing that one or more representatives from their own country should be sent over to control the manufacture; but as in all probability the demands for stamps at the commencement would not be large, it appears to us that it would be better (in the first place at any rate) to try and utilize one or other of the controlling staffs which already exist, or failing this to employ some assistants from your own office for the purposes of control, seeing that by this means the Chinese Government would obtain absolutely the same security as if they employed their own officers of control. In the event of the consumption of stamps increasing, the Chinese Government could then if they pleased send their own representatives to take charge of the manufacture, and after the whole had been thoroughly organized and established here, it might become worth while for them to consider whether or not they would transfer the manufacture to their own country. We, however, incline to the belief that upon thorough investigation, the very difficult conditions of the work would decide them not to adopt such a course, seeing that even if our best workmen could be induced to go to China, they would not, we are sure, produce anything like the same quality of work that they do with us, for apart from the climatic difficulties which would undoubtedly occur, of which would render the printing inks and other things concerned in the manufacture quite unmanageable the lack of our personal supervision would inevitably tell very seriously against them. Independently of a reluctance on our part to assume a tone of self-laudation, we cannot here attempt to lay before you the very great difficulties inseparable from the stamp manufacture, such difficulties as are only to be overcome by the accumulated teachings of long experience added to very close personal attention on our part. That there exist such difficult conditions as we indicate will, we think, be apparent to you from the consideration that amongst the thousands of printing establishments which exist in England, ours is the only one in which such stamps as are under consideration are produced.

Should the Chinese Authorities decide upon employing us, and at the same time should they not approve of our designs, it would be well if they could have designs prepared for us to work to, and further if they would for each duty of stamp required send us all the characters which would have to appear upon the face thereof, written with clearness in black upon white paper or cardboard; moreover, it would be an advantage if such characters were to be written in duplicate or even in triplicate. Besides this, it would be well if an estimate could be formed of the probable annual consumption of each value of stamp or Postage Envelope. We would strongly recommend that the initial order should bespeak a stock sufficient to last for three years (i.e. one year's supply for use and two years' supply for stock) seeing that in the case of India it is found necessary that a stock of two years' consumption should be always maintained there; otherwise there is a danger of its becoming exhausted before we can replenish it. This arises partly from the delay which takes place in the order reaching us; partly on account of the tedious processes through which the stamps have to pass before completion; and partly from the time consumed in their transit to India.

We trust you will not consider that we have allowed this letter to run to too great a length, but our wish to lay the matter before you in its principal bearings must be our apology for having entered into it so fully as we have done.

In conclusion, we beg to express our acknowledgments to the authorities concerned for their courtesy in supplying us with the specimens requisite to compile the Appendices to this letter, so important to the elucidation of the matter therein discussed.

We have the honour to be, Sir,
Your obedient servants,
Thomas De La Rue & Co.

James Duncan Campbell Esq.,
8 Storey's Gate, S.W.

1877 年 6 月 21 日金登干致德纳罗函

London Office of the Inspectorate General of
Chinese Imperial Maritime Customs:
8, Storey's Gate, St. James's Park, S.W.
21st June 1877

My dear Sir,

I have to thank you for your trade catalogue; and, I have no doubt, I shall have occasion, sooner or later, to apply to your firm for some of the supplies required by the authorities in China.

Yours truly,

J.D. Campbell

W.W. De La Rue Esq.

中国海关总税务司署伦敦办事处订货单一

London Office of the Inspectorate-General of
Chinese Maritime Customs

INDENT No.   REQUISITION No.

TENDER............................

............................hereby offer to supply (subject to inspection) of the best quality and make, free on board ship in............................, within the shortest time that can be named with certainty from the date of order, the articles hereinafter specified, at the price set against each, making together the sum of £............................. Abating all discounts or commissions.

Signature ....

Address ....

Dated..........this..........day of..........18

To THE SECRETARY
  8, Storey's Gate, St. James's Park, S.W.

DETAILED DESCRIPTION OF ARTICLE :

Harrild & Sons New Patent
Treadle "Bremner" Platter Machines, Demy Folio,
fitted with hand power. One extra ink-duct to be supplied with
each Machine, and fitted so as to be readily changed.

Quantity : 3

中国海关总税务司署伦敦办事处订货单二

London Office of the Inspectorate-General of

Chinese Maritime Customs

INDENT No.   REQUISITION No.

                 TENDER............................

..............................hereby offer to supply (subject to inspection) of the best quality and make, free on board ship in..........................., within the shortest time that can be named with certainty from the date of order, the articles hereinafter specified, at the price set against each, making together the sum of £........................... Abating all discounts or commissions.

Signature ....

Address ....

Dated........this........day of........18

To THE SECRETARY

     8, Storey's Gate, St. James's Park, S.W.

DETAILED DESCRIPTION OF ARTICLE :

Harrild & Sons   Best quality
Improved Round Hole Perforating Machines
25 ins wide

The above Perforating Machines are not to be supplied, if a Machine can be made to perforate more than one row at a time, a sheet of the exact size & design of the perforations to be made is enclosed.

Quantity : 2

中国海关总税务司署伦敦办事处订货单三

London Office of the Inspectorate-General of

Chinese Maritime Customs

INDENT No.   REQUISITION No.

TENDER...........................

...........................hereby offer to supply (subject to inspection) of the
best quality and make, free on board ship in..........................., within
the shortest time that can be named with certainty from the date of
order, the articles hereinafter specified, at the price set against each,
making together the sum of £........................... Abating all discounts or
commissions.

Signature ....

Address ....

Dated..........this..........day of..........18

To THE SECRETARY

8, Storey's Gate, St. James's Park, S.W.

DETAILED DESCRIPTION OF ARTICLE:

20 lbs : Lemon Yellow Ink

    （No. 3 in Specimen Book）

20 lbs : Mauve Ink

    （No. 15 in Specimen Book）

20 lbs : Chocolate Ink

    （No. 2 in Specimen Book）

20 lbs : Crimson Hake Ink

    （No. 13 in Specimen Book）

20 lbs : Bright Green Ink

    （No. 9 in Specimen Book）

10 lbs : Deep Orange Ink

    （No. 5 in Specimen Book）

中国海关总税务司署伦敦办事处订货单四

London Office of the Inspectorate-General of

Chinese Maritime Customs

INDENT No.   REQUISITION No.

TENDER...........................

...........................hereby offer to supply (subject to inspection) of the best quality and make, free on board ship in..........................., within the shortest time that can be named with certainty from the date of order, the articles hereinafter specified, at the price set against each, making together the sum of £........................... Abating all discounts or commissions.

Signature ....

Address ....

Dated.........this.........day of.........18

To THE SECRETARY

8, Storey's Gate, St. James's Park, S.W.

DETAILED DESCRIPTION OF ARTICLE :

600 Reams, of 500 Sheets each, of handmade paper, suitable for Postage Stamps, of the size & design of the accompanying sheet, with the water mark of a rising sun on each square.

The above paper must be forwarded as soon as possible, say 50 reams at a time.

Quantity : 600

中国海关总税务司署伦敦办事处订货单五

London Office of the Inspectorate-General of

Chinese Maritime Customs

INDENT No.   REQUISITION No.

TENDER............................

............................hereby offer to supply (subject to inspection) of the
best quality and make, free on board ship in............................, within
the shortest time that can be named with certainty from the date of
order, the articles hereinafter specified, at the price set against each,
making together the sum of £............................ Abating all discounts or
commissions.

Signature ....
Address ....
Dated..........this..........day of..........18

To THE SECRETARY

8, Storey's Gate, St. James's Park, S.W.

DETAILED DESCRIPTION OF ARTICLE :

25 Gallons of specially prepared Gum or Composition for gumming Postage Stamps, a damp climate to be taken into consideration.

The above composition must be supplied by monthly instalments of two gallons. If the ingredients can be attained for mixing here it will be advisable to forward them dry.

Quantity : 25

中国海关总税务司署伦敦办事处订货单六

London Office of the Inspectorate-General of
Chinese Maritime Customs

INDENT No.   REQUISITION No.

TENDER............................

........................hereby offer to supply (subject to inspection) of the
best quality and make, free on board ship in........................, within
the shortest time that can be named with certainty from the date of
order, the articles hereinafter specified, at the price set against each,
making together the sum of £........................ Abating all discounts or
commissions.

Signature ....
Address ....
Dated..........this..........day of..........18

To THE SECRETARY
    8, Storey's Gate, St. James's Park, S.W.

DETAILED DESCRIPTION OF ARTICLE :

Letter Scales of the largest size the same as are used in the British Post office.

Quantity : 20

Letter Scales of the smallest size the same as are used in the British Post Office.

Quantity : 30

Both sizes to be provided with Postal Union weights. (Grammes)

1877 年 7 月 5 日金登干致德纳罗函

London Office of the Inspectorate General of

Chinese Imperial Maritime Customs:

8, Storey's Gate, St. James's Park, S.W.

In reply please refer to

No. 2475

And address to the J.

Secretary

Chinese Customs' Office

5th July 1877

Dear Sir,

Referring to our conversation of yesterday, I now enclose copy of the telegram I sent to the Inspector General.

The French Steamer, bringing the next mails from China has been wrecked and the mails have been lost. I fear that the promised memorandum, explanatory of the Requisitions already received and of those that were to follow may have been despatched by this Steamer - otherwise, it will no doubt be forthcoming by the English mail due here on the 16th instant.

From the Requisitions, however, which I have submitted to your criticism, you may perhaps be able to form some opinion of the scale upon which the Inspector General contemplates commencing the production of the postage stamps in China, and to estimate, accordingly, for the machinery and appliances that would be required there - supposing that the Inspector General prefers making the stamps on the spot to having them manufactured in England.

In this connection, it may be necessary to consider which of the several processes will be the best and adopted for the climate and for the resources possessed by the Customs' printing Establishment at Shanghai.

I wish, however, to be prepared to execute the order with the utmost dispatch, in the event of the Inspector General telegraphing back instructions to supply the Stores in accordance with several Requisitions that have been prepared in China.

I am, Dear Sir,

Yours truly,

J.D. Campbell

W.W. De La Rue Esq.

1877 年 7 月 5 日金登干致德纳罗函附件

Copy of telegram from Mr. Campbell to Mr. Hart,
dated 4th July 1877

"Postal Requisitions impracticable. Machine, Paper, Ink all unsuitable. Elaborate report mailed 22nd June. If you send immediately design for each stamp and, upon receipt report, telegraph instructions, all kinds can be delivered here ten weeks afterwards, price £54 per million. Special experience required, Time expense saved and protection from forgery ensured by starting manufacturing here - transferring to China afterwards."

1877 年 7 月 5 日德纳罗致金登干函

110 Bunhill Row, E.C.

July 5th, 1877

Sir,

We should feel reluctant to tender for the machines and other things included in the Requisitions which you send us upon the 2nd, inst., seeing, that in our view they are quite unsuitable for the purpose for which they are required, viz. for the manufacture of postage stamps. The "Bremner platen" is a very good machine for common type printing, but it is neither sufficiently powerful, nor in any way calculated to produce stamps, and, in fact, it is really only adapted for the purpose for which it has been specially devised, viz for "jobbing" printing.

We should not like to provide you with one of Messrs. Harrild's Perforating Machines, seeing that Messrs. Napier's machines although somewhat higher in price are, as our experience has taught us, infinitely superior to those of any other makers. At the same time, a treadle Perforating Machine is hardly suitable for perforating a large quantity of stamps; for which it would be necessary, we think, to have the same form of machine as is employed by the Imperial Government at Somerset House.

The printing inks specified are those used for ordinary type printing, and are in no way suitable for stamp printing, seeing that when once such inks have become dry an obliteration can be removed from their surface without in any way destroying the print. Thus if stamps were printed in such inks, although they might be thoroughly obliterated they could very easily be cleaned and used a second time, without in any way revealing the fraud. It is, therefore, essential that stamps should be printed in none other than "fugitive" inks.

The hand-made paper about which enquiry is made would not be suitable for stamp printing, seeing that any paper which could be made by hand would be far too harsh for the reception of a fine print. When first we commenced the stamp manufacture, the paper-making machine had not been brought to anything like the perfection which has since been arrived at, and we had consequently at that time (we are speaking of 30 or 40 years ago) to employ hand-made paper for the stamps, but so soon as we could obtain a satisfactory water-mark in machine-made paper, we at once abandoned that made by hand, seeing that the printing upon it was always unsatisfactory and attended with great difficulties. Apart from this consideration, the fact that it is impossible to ensure uniform thickness in hand-made paper is another argument against its employment for the particular purpose in question, for if the paper vary in thickness the appearance of the prints taken upon it will also vary, seeing that if thinner or thicker paper than that for which the press is adjusted be used either the impression will be too light or too heavy, thus imparting a very different appearance to the stamps. Now, it is important that stamps should not only be inherently good but uniform in appearance, so that the users thereof may be able to recognize a genuine stamp without hesitation.

The paper should be prepared on one side and then gummed before printing, so that it would not be necessary to supply any gum or composition, but we fear that if an attempt were made to send out gummed paper to China it might possibly be injuriously affected by moisture, even though it were packed in tin-lined cases.

As you will gather by the above remarks, we are of opinion that the machinery and appliances which have been indented for are altogether unfit for the purpose for which they are required. We fully appreciate, however, the difficulty which must have been experienced by the framer of the Requisition (in consequence of his being unfamiliar with the special conditions to be fulfilled)in the selection of such things as might appear necessary for the production of stamps, and we think that under the circumstances he could not well have made a better choice.

We are in hopes that the Chinese Government will decide to avail themselves of our experience in the Postage Stamp manufacture, for it appears to us to be of the very first importance that the stamps which they employ should be of such a nature as to inspire confidence, seeing that should they be insecure it would inevitably result that they would be freely forged in China, and that consequently the whole system of collecting revenue by means of stamps would be discredited, whereas if stamps were issued such as would be secure against forgery, there is every probability that the system would extend beyond that of the postal service, and that in time a vast revenue would be collected through the agency of stamps as is the case in India. That these conclusions are well founded is shown by what has taken place in the latter country. When some thirty years ago, we were first applied to by the Government of India to manufacture stamps, their use was practically limited to the postage service; but since that time we have been employed for the production of a great variety of Indian stamps, by means of which very large revenues are collected annually, and there is no doubt whatever that the reason for the extension of the system is that confidence is felt in the security of the stamps, and that if such confidence were lacking their use would have been limited almost to what it was formerly. We refer to India more particularly because it appears to us that the conditions there and in China are somewhat similar, seeing that the natives of both countries are renowned for their patience and skill as copyists but the same arguments would apply in the case of England and many other countries which we have supplied with stamps, excepting that in a more highly civilized land there would appear to be other checks for the protection of the government, besides the actual security of the stamps. That is not, however, any reason why secure stamps should not be employed and the English Government has always found it advantageous to obtain from us those of the highest character. These considerations, and those into which we entered so fully in our letter of the 18th ulto., will, we have no doubt, convince the authorities concerned in initiating the Postal System in China of the advantage to be derived from employing for their purpose stamps of the highest class which can be obtained, viz. those produced by our improved system.

We have the honour to be, Sir,
Your obedt. servants,
W.W. De La Rue

J.D. Campbell Esq.
& Storey's Gale, S.W.

No. 2483   London Office of the Inspectorate General of
Chinese Maritime Customs:
8, Storey's Gate, St. James's Park, S.W.

6th July 1877

Gentlemen,

I beg to acknowledge the receipt of your letter of yesterday's date and to thank you for the observations, you have been so good as to favour me to write, upon the Postal Requisitions referred to you on the 2nd instant.

I am quite of your opinion that gummed paper would be injuriously affected by moisture, during transport to China, and I would enquire, therefore, whether it would not be possible to make the gum composition on the spot, if the necessary materials were sent out.

I shall be glad to hear from Mr. W.W. De La Rue (in reply to the letter I addressed him yesterday) whether, taking into consideration the circumstances under which the Requisitions were prepared in China, he could suggest any way of meeting the requirements and enabling the Customs' printing establishment at Shanghai to commence the production of postage stamps on the 1st of October next.

I am,

Gentlemen,

Your obedient Servant,

J.D. Campbell

Messrs. De La Rue & Co.

Bunhill Row,

E.C.

1877 年 7 月 6 日德纳罗致金登干函

My dear sir,

I am much obliged to you for your letter of yesterday, and for the copy of the telegram which it enclosed. I infer from what you say that you propose to await an answer to this telegram before taking any action in the matter, and this would certainly seem the best course. So soon as you receive a further communication from China, I shall be glad to see you upon the subject; for if, notwithstanding all the arguments against such a course the Inspector General decides to print the stamps in China, he must of course be furnished with the proper means of doing so, & we should be happy to lend you every assistance in the matter. I am in hopes, however, that he will decide to have the manufacture at least initiated by us.

You will no doubt have received our formal letter of yesterday.

Yours very truly

W.W. De La Rue

P.T.O.

J.D. Campbell Esq.

P.S. Your letter of this morning is just to hand, and we should of course have to try and make some gumming composition which could be sent to China, should it be decided to manufacture the stamps there, but even in this case the paper would have to have a coat of preparation before it was sent.

As I have such said above, if, after all, it is decided that the stamps must be manufactured in China, we should be happy to assist you as far as possible, but we hope that the Inspector-General will come to a wiser conclusion. I suppose, however, nothing can be done until you receive a telegram from China, or do you think any of the matters——such as the dies and printing plates——might be put in hand at once.

In compliance with the request conveyed through your messenger, I return you the diagram which accompanied your Requisition forms.

1877 年 12 月 17 日金登干致德纳罗函

Indent No. 193   London Office of the Inspectorate General of

Chinese Maritime Customs:

8, Storey's Gate, St. James's Park, S.W.

17th Dec 1877

Gentlemen,

You are invited to forward to this office, as soon as possible, a tender on the enclosed form (*in Duplicate*) for the articles specified therein. [Tender/In Duplicate]

Should you not be inclined to contract for the same, you are requested to be good enough to return the form (*in Duplicate*) to this office at your earliest convenience.

I am,

Your obedient Servant,

J.D. Campbell

Secretary.

To

Messrs. De La Rue & Co.

Bunhill Row,

E.C.

CHINESE IMPERIAL MARITIME CUSTOMS

INDENT No.193   Shanghai   REQUISITION No.19

Duplicate

Tender for Cloth boards for binding books

We hereby offer to supply (subject to inspection) of the best quality and make, free on board ship in London, within seven weeks from the date of order, the articles hereinafter specified, at the price set against each, making together the sum of £56"3"4 net cash.

Signature: W.W. De La Rue & Co.

Address: 110 Bunhill Row, London, EC

Dated: this 19th day of December 1877

Detailed Description of Article :

One thousand dark green cloth boards, to contain 37 sheets (folded in quarto) of the toned demy of which specimen is enclosed. The outside of front cover to bear a stamp in gilt, in facsimile of the Chinese characters at the head of the title page enclosed, the back to be lettered.

Le Saint Edit

A.T. Piry

Shanghai

Bureau des Statistiques

Douanes Impériales

Remarks :

Both sides to have a handsome blind border and the first side the Chinese letters in gold in addition. The back to be worked in gold & blind.

The sides to be stamped with some neat & appropriate design for a border.

N.B. These covers are wanted in China at the earliest possible date.

Quantity : 1000

Amount : £54/3/4

Total Cost of Articles : £54/3/4

Packing in best manner for shipment : £2

Net Amount, payable on Receipt of

Bills of Lading from Shipping Agents. : £56/3/4

1877 年 12 月 21 日订货函

Order No. 193   London Office of the Inspectorate General of

Chinese Maritime Customs:

8, Storey's Gate, St. James's Park, S.W.

21st December 1877

Gentlemen,

I have to request that you will supply the 1000 dark green cloth boards in accordance with you tender of the 19th instant.

I will thank you to acknowledge the receipt of this letter and to notify me when the stores are ready for inspection.

I am,

Gentlemen,

Your obedient Servant,

F.E. Taylor

pro

Secretary

To

Messrs. Thos. De La Rue & Co.

110 Bunhill Row,

E.C.

December 22nd 7

Sir,

We have to thank you for your letter of yesterday, accepting our Tender of the 19th inst, for the supply of 1000 dark green Cloth Boards. This order shall have our immediate attention.

We understand that you require us to send in a duplicate of our Tender, but as we thought that the duplicate form you furnished us with was intended for our own use we have fastened it in a book. This being the case, we should feel much obliged if you would kindly send us another form, which we will duly fill in and return to you.

We have the honour to be, Sir,
Your obedient Servants,
W.W. De La Rue

J.D. Campbell Esq.,
8 Storey's Gate,
St. James's Park.

1877 年 12 月 24 日函

MEMORANDUM

Reference No.3176   24 Dec. 1877

(To be quoted in reply.)

From The Secretary.   To Messrs. De La Rue & Co.

London Office of Chinese Imperial Maritime Customs,

   8, STOREY'S GATE, ST. JAMES'S PARK, S.W.

In accordance with your request, a duplicate form of tender is
herewith enclosed, which you are requested to sign and return to
this office.

1878 年 1 月 22 日海关伦敦办事处函

London Office of the Inspectorate General of

Chinese Maritime Customs,

8, STOREY'S GATE, ST. JAMES'S PARK, S.W.

22 January, 1878

ORDER No. 193

For Cloth Board Covers

Gentlemen,

1. Marking Instructions

With reference to the Stores supplied by you under Order No.193, you are requested to have the cases, &c., marked in accordance with the printed directions enclosed, and numbered from No.1 upwards.

2. Schedule of Packages in duplicate

Shipping Instructions will be sent to you, upon your returning to this office, properly filled up in duplicate, the enclosed Schedules of Packages, showing the Nos., description, weight, measurement, value, &c., of each Case or Package in detail, for the purposes of shipment and insurance.

3. Packing Accounts in triplicate

You are also requested to return, as soon as possible, the enclosed packing accounts, properly filled up in duplicate, showing the contents of each case or package in detail; and to forward, at the same time, your monied Invoices in triplicate, the items being entered therein in the same order in which they are stated in your Tender. Payment of the same will be made upon receipt of the

Bills of Lading from the Shipping agent.

I am,

Gentlemen,

Your obedient Servant,

J.D. CAMPBELL,

Secretary.

To

Messrs. Thos. De La Rue & Co.

110 Bunhill Row, E.C.

(Entered Export Day Book Folio A)

London Office of the Inspectorate General of Chinese Maritime Customs.
DIRECTIONS FOR MARKING CASES, &c.

The Cases should be marked in accordance with this Diagram bearing the distinctive mark of the Chinese Imperial Maritime Customs ☯ on the top of each case, the destination on the front, and a general description of the contents n the left side, for the guidance of the authorities in China.

Casks and all other Pieces and Packages should be similarly marked as far as possible, and where the nature of the Package will not allow of its being marked, Labels, properly addressed as above, should be securely fastened to it as shown in the following drawing of a Coil of Wire.

The Label is placed inside the Coil to protect the address from abrasion.

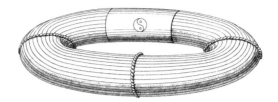

Note.—The Mark is constructed by describing two equal semi-circles ⟨ with a circle round them, thus:- ☯ the right side of the figure is dark, having the centre or eye of the upper semi-circle bright, whilst the left side is bright and the eye dark.

档案原本

May 1st 77

1. What would . say . one million postage stamps made in England cost? £506 2&0

2. What would it cost to procure machinery, plant and paper to make in China say one million stamps per week? impracticable

3. What would be the cost per month of the English personnel required for producing one million stamps a week, taking into consideration that all elementary manual labour can be had here. Will write from report.

Yellow Imperial Colour
Red Pink Happy
Blue Mourning
green Happy
Brown Mourning

Mr. James Duncan Campbell
Commissioner of Customs China
London Office of the Inspectorate General
of Chinese Maritime Customs
2 Kings Gate St. Westminster St. S.W.

丽如银行的钱币照片与"龙"图

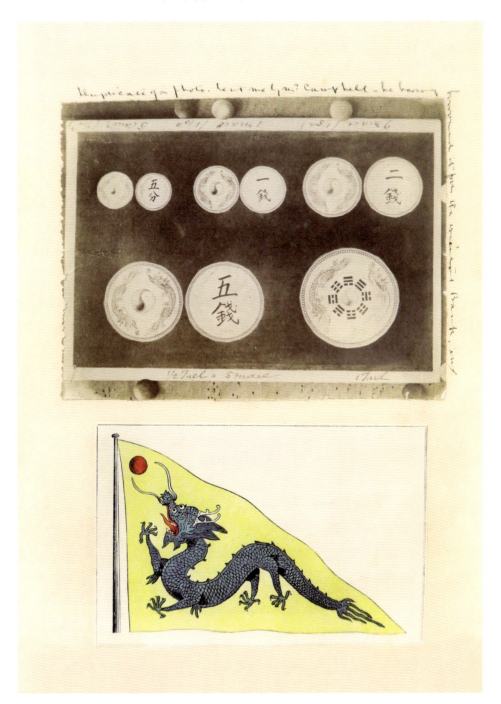

LONDON OFFICE OF THE INSPECTORATE GENERAL OF
CHINESE IMPERIAL MARITIME CUSTOMS.

8, STOREY'S GATE, ST JAMES'S PARK, S.W.

22 May. 1877

W.W.D.
24 MAY 77
FOL.46/C.18.

Dear Sir,

I enclose two sketches I received from Peking some time ago.

In the Ying & Yang device, the dark side should be uppermost ☯. I also send you a sketch of a dragon on a large scale.

I shall be glad if you

269

will let me have your
report before next mail
day (Friday) as I telegraphed
to China that details
would be ready last
Friday.

Yours,

JD. Campbell.

P.S.

Will you kindly return the
two small sketches, when
you have done with them

JDC.

8, Storey's Gate, St James's Park. S.W.

23 May/77

My dear Sir,

In each of the two small sketches I sent you yesterday, there is a globe, floating in space, which is intended for the "Zin

June 8ᵗʰ 1877.

Memo.

In my second interview with Mr. Campbell, on my 3rd, I explained to him that we only do business with English houses, and that we should, therefore, hesitate to supply the Chinese Government direct. He, however, told me that the Oriental Bank would be prepared upon the occasion of each order which might reach us through him to vouch for the payment of the amount entailed.

Confidential.

110 Bunhill Row,
London, E.C.,
June 8th 1877

Sir,

We have before us, together with your answers thereto, the telegram which you recently received from the Inspector General of Chinese Maritime Customs; and in fulfilment of our promise we will now, with your permission, proceed to give you such information as may be requisite to enable you to furnish a Report upon the subject of Adhesive Stamps to that gentleman.

We will in this letter chiefly confine ourselves to Stamps which are used for the Postage Service, seeing that it is they with which you are immediately concerned, but we will, with your permission, before closing also give such particulars about Revenue, Customs or Law Stamps as will show the conditions which they have to fulfil.

Adhesive Stamps are produced upon four different systems, viz:—

(A.) By the intaglio printing process.
(B.) By the lithographic printing process.
(C.) By the embossing process, that being generally combined with one or other of the printing processes.
(D.) By the surface-printing process.

James Duncan Campbell Esq,
8 Storey's Gate, S.W.

275

We will deal with the processes in the order in which they are given; but before entering into the matter, we should explain that the various specimens of Stamps to which we shall refer as being given in our Appendices have advisedly been overprinted with the word "Cancelled" in order to destroy them.

(A.) — In the intaglio printing process, the configuration of the Stamp is recessed into a steel die by means of a knife-like instrument termed a "graver". Supposing, for example, it were wished to print the letter A in the process in question, the lines requisite to form that letter would have to be cut or scratched into a steel die to a depth, which would be about equal to the thickness of the paper on which we write. In order to print the letter from such a die, printing ink, consisting of boiled linseed oil mixed with any coloured pigment which might be required (e.g. blue, red, green, yellow, &c. &c.) would have to be rubbed over the die with a piece of rag, the effect being that the whole surface of the die would be smeared over with the printing ink, and that it would lodge itself in the recesses forming the letter A, so that when in the next operation a clean piece of rag were taken and rubbed to and fro over the surface of the die, so as to remove the printing ink from it, that which had lodged in the recesses would not be disturbed. We should then have a die with a perfectly clean surface, but with the incised letter A filled with printing ink,

2.

and it is obvious that if by any means, we could, so arrange as to convey the printing ink from the recesses in the die to the surface of a piece of paper, we should have a printed letter A. This result is effected by laying a piece of paper upon the die, and passing the two together between rollers which are so contrived as to press the paper with considerable force against the die. As the printing ink has a greater affinity or kindness for the paper than for the metal, so soon as the paper is pressed sufficiently close to the die to bring the surface of the former in contact with the ink, which is in the recesses of the latter the ink clings to the paper and accompanies it when removed from the die, rather than remain in its recesses. Such is an outline of the method of intaglio printing, and it will be readily understood that the same explanation would apply whether the form of the print were merely that of a simple letter A or whether it were of an elaborate character, like the intaglio printed stamps at the top of our Appendix A., each line of which represents a recess in the plate.

The stamps are not, of course, printed singly, but in considerable numbers. In this country, there are generally as many as 240 stamps to a sheet, seeing that there are 240 units of our currency (i.e. pence) in the pound; besides which a sheet containing 240 Postage Stamps is a very convenient size to manufacture. It should be understood that the 240 stamps which are printed on a sheet are not obtained by taking 240 separate

3.

277

impressions upon different parts of the sheet from a printing die or plate containing only one stamp, but from a printing plate containing as many repeats of the stamps as have to appear in the printed sheet. Nevertheless, the engraver has only to cut or engrave one stamp. The small plate or die on which he does so is termed the original and becomes the parent of the full sized plates used to print from, and, which, as before stated, generally contain 240 multiples of the stamp. These working plates are obtained from the original die by means of an apparatus, which it would be difficult to describe without diagrams. Suffice it to say that a soft steel roller is passed under great pressure to and fro over the original die until the metal of the roller has been squeezed into the recesses of the die, the effect being that exact counterparts of the recesses in the die are formed in relief upon the roller. After such a roller had been hardened by being plunged at a red heat into cold water, it would if rolled with pressure over a metallic plate furnish a facsimile of the original die, seeing that the projections in the roller would make corresponding depressions in the plate under treatment. Not only may one impression be taken from the roller in this manner, but any number may be obtained by repeating the like process, so long as the roller remains in good condition, and of its deterioration there is not much fear,

4.

seeing that it is brought to a great hardness before being used. But even if it should wear out, nothing more would be necessary than to revert to the original die in order to obtain a new roller. Consequently, we have the means of making any number of facsimiles of the original die; and by the aid of certain appliances we are enabled to make these in plates of metal at equal distances apart so as to form working plates of 240 or any less number of multiples.

(B). — For the lithographic printing process, the original die is prepared in exactly the same manner as in that for intaglio printing; but instead of its being multiplied in order to form working plates in the manner above described, prints are taken from it upon "transfer paper". This consists of ordinary paper dressed with a preparation of starch so as to form a soluble film upon its surface. The print is taken on this film, and whilst still wet it is laid face downwards upon a polished slab of lithographic stone. This kind of stone has an affinity for a greasy substance like printing ink, and when the print is laid on it the stone is well disposed towards the ink to which it is thus introduced. As, however, the object is not only to bring the print into contact with the stone, but actually to transfer it from the paper to the stone, the paper is slightly damped at the back, so that the soluble film which is on its surface may be acted upon by the water. As soon as

5.

the paper has been sufficiently moistened, it is forcibly pressed against the stone by passing it under a special form of press. The consequence of this operation is that the print is brought into very close contact with the stone, whilst the soluble film, having been disengaged from the paper, and having consequently thrown off the ink therefrom, the latter clings to the stone as a matter of necessity. We have thus a somewhat porous stone with a printed impression upon its surface, which, being oleaginous, will resist water, at the same time having an affinity for printing ink, that being of a greasy nature. If, therefore, a sponge charged with water be passed over the stone, those parts thereof which are unprinted will absorb moisture, whilst the printed parts will throw off or resist the water. Consequently, if a roller charged with printing ink (composed of boiled linseed oil and pigment) be passed over the stone so moistened, the printing ink will adhere to the greasy pattern upon the stone, but will not adhere to the bare portion thereof by reason of the moisture thereon. We should have explained that before the stone is actually printed from, the transferred pattern is fixed thereto by the application of an acid solution which has the effect of setting the pattern firmly to the stone, so that it may be printed from without injury. When a layer of printing ink has been imparted to the pattern in the manner described, all that is necessary to obtain a printed impression is to lay a sheet of paper upon the stone and to pass it through the press. By this means, the paper is brought into close contact with the face of the stone, and the printing ink which has been spread over the pattern by means of the roller, is pressed on to the paper, so that when the sheet is lifted from the stone it is found to be printed with the desired pattern. By way of illustration we give on Appendix A. a specimen of a stamp printed by the process under consideration.

It will be understood that 240 or any other number of stamps can be obtained on a sheet by merely taking the requisite number of single prints on transfer paper from the original die, and laying them down at the proper distance from one another upon the stone before the back of the transfer paper is damped as above described. Thus, any number of stamps can be transferred to a stone in like manner as the single one we have considered.

(C). As we have already stated, the embossing process of producing Postage Stamps is generally combined with one or other of the printing processes. As, however, we are dealing with the printing processes separately we will not here consider their application to embossed stamps, seeing that it will be sufficient to describe the manner in which the embossment is made, since when once the printing processes are understood it is only necessary to conceive that one or other of them has been resorted to before embossing a stamp to understand clearly the manner in which it has been produced. As will be seen by the specimens of embossed stamps in Appendix A; it is usual to confine the embossment to the central figure of the stamp, leaving the rest of the configuration to be carried out by printing; nevertheless, there would be no difficulty in extending the area of embossment were it so desired. The process is as follows:— A soft steel block or die is taken and the head or other device to be embossed is scooped out of it by means of hardened steel tools. So soon as the pattern has been completed, the die is hardened, in the manner described in connection with the first process, and impressions are taken from it in square leaden blocks of the size of a stamp by means of a fly-press, there being a special contrivance to keep the blocks exactly square, even when they are subjected to such a pressure as is requisite to make the lead flow into the recesses of the steel die, so as to form a perfect counterpart thereof. 240 of such leads, or a number corresponding to the multiples required in the working plate, are struck with the die, and they are then grouped together

8.

with accuracy so as to form an exact counterpart of the plate which is required, excepting that those parts which will be sunken in the plate project in the leads. The leads thus arranged are placed in the trough of a battery, so that a copper counterpart of them may be produced by the electrotyping process. This copper counterpart when removed from the leads constitutes the working plate, and in fact contains as many exact duplicates of the original die as there were leads. After it has been mounted by being screwed down to a plate of iron, it is put under a powerful fly-press, having a thick sheet of warm gutta percha laid on the top of it; the press is now put in action, by which repeated blows are applied to the gutta percha, so as to drive it into the recesses of the plate. When the gutta percha has thus been forced into every recess of the plate, the former is lifted off the latter and fastened coincidently with the plate to the upper slab of the fly-press. The sheet of stamps to be embossed, having already been printed, is then laid face downwards upon the plate and visited with a heavy blow from the press, the gutta percha counterpart coming down with the upper slab thereof and forcing the paper into every recess of the plate. Thus, when it is removed from the plate and turned face upwards, those parts which were driven into the recesses of the plate are found to be raised or embossed to a height proportionate

9.

to the depth of the recesses which they occupied.

Now each of these three processes for the production of stamps is open to very grave objection, not only because they lack refinement, and consequently produce but comparatively clumsy work, but what is of more importance the stamps produced thereby can not only be forged but can be cleaned from a printed obliteration, and so fraudulently used a second time. It will be understood from what has gone before that in printing upon the intaglio system the printing ink is left in ridges upon the paper. These ridges are very apparent when the ink is wet, and although they are much reduced in height by the shrinking of the ink in the process of drying, it is evident (although the difference can hardly be detected by the naked eye) that the stamp must remain thicker in the printed portions than in the plain, seeing that the whole of the ink which filled the recesses in the plate passed to the paper in the form of ridges. This condition offers very great facilities to the forger, for its existence renders it possible to produce absolute facsimiles of the printing plate in the following manner. A certain preparation of wax and asphaltum, called etching-ground, is applied to the surface of a steel or copper plate in a thin layer and allowed to set hard. The intaglio printed stamp to be dealt with is then laid face downwards upon the prepared side of the plate and the two together are passed through

10.

284

a pair of pressure rollers, the effect being that the ridges of the print press into the etching-grounds and by reason of its brittleness break it up. The plate is then treated with acid, which attacks the portions that have been exposed through the fracture of the etching-ground, whilst where this has been left intact, or in other words in those parts where no ridges of print have fallen, the metal is protected from the action of the acid. The ridges of an intaglio plate may in fact be considered as almost equivalent to knife-edges cutting through the protecting mantle which is put upon the plate, thereby exposing it in those parts where they fall to the action of the acid. Thus although the ridges cannot be brought actually to indent the metallic plate, it is possible through their agency to obtain in an indirect manner counterparts of the ridges, or in other words to reproduce the original plate from which they were printed; the depth of the indentations in the forged plate depending of course upon the length of time during which the action of the acid may be maintained. As we have shown you, we have in this manner produced copies of intaglio stamp printing plates, so exact that it is impossible to distinguish the forged stamps printed with them from the true ones.

This particular mode of forgery is applicable only to intaglio printed stamps, for in them alone is the pattern produced in ridges of printing ink, seeing that both in the lithographic process and the surface printing process, which we will presently describe, the ink is merely laid on the paper superficially, that is to say in so thin a layer that it rises to no appreciable height. The lithographic process is, however, very unsuitable for stamp printing, the prints being unavoidably ill-defined or blurred instead of being sharp and distinct — so essential for real security — besides which stamps printed by that process, as well as those printed by the intaglio process, are exposed to forgery by a method very much simpler than that above described. The success of the transfer processes of forgery depends upon certain properties possessed by the drying oils, one of which (linseed oil) is of necessity used for printing ink. Although after exposure to the air printing ink becomes hard, still be it ever so dry it only has to be soaked in a dilute solution of hydrochloric acid to make it assume almost its original viscid condition. If a dry print be taken, and be subjected to such treatment, it is brought to very much the same condition as when first printed; and if it be laid on a lithographic stone and passed through a press, a portion of the softened ink will adhere to the stone, sufficient to enable a skilful operator by careful

12.

286

manipulation to bring the pattern thus made upon the stone into a fit condition to print from. That is the ordinary process of forgery by transfer, but a very much more refined one is available, by which very faithful copies of intaglio or lithographic printed stamps can be obtained, seeing that with a good pattern upon the stone the lithographer is capable of producing impressions which would well pass for intaglio prints, and he can of course with a proper pattern upon the stone copy stamps produced originally by his branch of the printing art. In the process we allude to instead of depending upon the peculiar behaviour of the printing ink when subjected to the action of dilute hydrochloric acid, the affinity which the printing ink has for an oleaginous substance is turned to account. The stamp to be operated upon is immersed in a cup of water and left to soak until the water has penetrated the substance of the paper, when it sinks to the bottom of the cup. A little oil is then floated upon the surface of the water and the stamp is by means of a pair of tweezers brought in a diagonal direction face upwards through the layer of oil, the action being that while the wet paper repels the oil, the kindly printing ink upon its surface receives a layer thereof. As a consequence, the plain portions of the stamp are left perfectly clean, whilst the printed portion has a layer of oil

13.

287

on its surface, which can be readily transferred to a lithographic stone, so that a very perfect pattern from which to print is obtained, seeing that the oil has sufficient affinity for the stone to cling to it readily.

With the embossing process, the forger would have if anything even less difficulty than with the intaglio or lithographic printing process. His plan of operation would be to support a stamp underneath with plaster of Paris, or some other suitable material, and then to take a cast from it as a first step to a copy in metal. This could easily be obtained by the electrotype process, or indeed by a variety of methods, and it would yield any number of paper impressions which might be required.

In addition to these inherent defects in the processes which have been under review, there are two other good reasons against their employment; the first being that they do not afford the means of printing the stamps in "fugitive" ink; and the second that the stamps produced by them are, independently of their liability to be forged, but imperfect productions. The consideration of the first-mentioned defect, we will postpone for the present; at the same time, we should point out that the intaglio printed stamps are not only clumsy in appearance, but that they are neither so clean nor so serviceable as they should

14.

be, seeing that the ink lying in ridges is likely to smudge with abrasion, which of necessity, must frequently happen in the handling of Postage Stamps no less than in their transit through the post. The lithographic stamps, as we have before stated, are altogether inferior in quality, whilst the embossed stamps are not only somewhat crude in themselves, but are very bulky in comparison with the others on account of the embossment, besides which they are liable to be flattened by pressure.

(D).— Now all these considerations have led us to discard the three processes which we have discussed above in favour of the improved surface stamp printing process, which we succeeded in perfecting some thirty years ago, and which is illustrated by the last group of specimens on Appendix A. This process is in fact now employed for almost all the stamps which we manufacture; and it enables us to produce stamps which are secure against forgery and are proof against being fraudulently cleaned and used a second time. It may almost be described as being the reverse of the intaglio process, seeing that instead of the pattern being cut or recessed in the original die, the die is so cut as to leave the pattern in relief. The printing or working plates are made from this relief die very much in the same manner, as the embossing working plates as described above, excepting, of course, that

15.

the final result is to obtain a working plate, with the pattern projected instead of being recessed. The process of printing consists in passing a special kind of roller charged with 'fugitive' printing ink over the working plate, so that those parts with which it comes in contact (i. e. the raised patterns) are charged with a mere superficies of ink. When a sheet of paper is laid upon this inked plate and is subjected to pressure (and the pressure is enormous, being produced by a special kind of press) the ink is transferred from the plate to the paper, by which means an exquisitely fine print is produced, seeing that great delicacy can be obtained in the original die, and as a consequence in the working plate, whilst a perfect impression of this plate can be made on the paper, and that too in such a manner that the pattern is in the same plane as the paper, not in ridges as in the case of the intaglio printed stamps. Consequently, the surface printed stamps are not only refined in appearance (a matter of the first moment), but they are secure against the process of forgery which depends for success upon the pattern being raised above the surface of the paper. The great importance of having stamps of a very refined character must be at once apparent by the reflection that the more perfect their nature, the more able are they to defy imitation

16.

by drawing, engraving, or any other such process,
for were. they not productions of a high character,
and indeed of their kind as perfect as are to be
obtained, a facility for their imitation would
offer itself to a skilful operator, even were it not
in his power to employ the stamps themselves
in any way as auxiliaries by either of the methods
of forgery discussed previously.

    We have now arrived at that point at
which it will be useful to show the conditions
which our fugitive inks have to fulfil. The
inks in question are termed fugitive because
they retreat or disappear under the attacks
of solvents such as could be used to remove
from a stamp a printed obliteration, that is
to say they are soluble in the hydro-carbons
and similar liquids. The intaglio and
lithographic printing processes do not
admit of the use of such inks, and as a
consequence stamps printed by either of
those processes are unaffected by the liquids
above referred to, and in fact they may when
dry be soaked in benzine (we take benzine
as the most convenient of the solvents which
could be used to clean stamps) for an
indefinite period without any result. Postage
stamps are cancelled by the impress of an
obliterating mark with a hand-stamp,
such a mark as is shown at the top of

17.

291

our Appendix B. The ink employed for that purpose is of a peculiar description termed "endorsing" ink, and when dry it has the property of being nearly insoluble in benzine. If, then, a stamp, printed in 'fugitive' ink be obliterated with the endorsing ink, the obliteration cannot be removed without destroying the stamp, as will be seen by referring to Appendix B. The second example is a 3. English Postage Stamp obliterated with "endorsing" ink and so left; the following one a stamp similarly obliterated, but subsequently treated with benzine. As will be seen the effect has been to destroy the stamp, whilst the obliteration is but little disturbed. Consequently, if stamps printed in such fugitive ink be efficiently cancelled by a printed obliteration, they cannot be cleansed for fraudulent use a second time, as they could be were the ink not of a fugitive character, as is exemplified by the intaglio printed stamps in Appendix B. These two stamps being printed in ordinary printing ink, the obliteration in the lower one has been almost entirely washed away, whilst the stamp has been left undisturbed. It will be understood that before it was treated with benzine, the lower example had exactly the same appearance as the upper one. It is, then, of the utmost importance

18.

that Postage Stamps should be printed in fugitive ink, so that the obliteration may be an efficient agent of destruction.

As we have before stated, this obliteration is usually imparted by means of a hand-stamp, but where large quantities of letters have to be dealt with, an obliterating machine supplied by us is used for the purpose, similar to that shown in the photograph at the top of Appendix C. This machine (worked by hand) is comparatively cheap, its cost being only £12 (exclusive of packing &c.) and is capable of obliterating a very great number of stamps in the course of a day. It is fitted with a stamp or a pair of stamps, as illustrated by the photographs in Appendices C. & D. One of these serves to obliterate the stamp with a secret symbol or combination of letters showing the office at which the obliteration took place, whilst the other being placed in the machine alongside its companion is impressed upon the body of the envelope and gives the name of the town at which the obliteration took place as well as the time and date thereof. The latter stamp cannot be considered as serving the purpose of an obliterating mark, but rather as a companion to the true obliterating mark. It, however, gives in one sense the most important part

19.

293

of the obliteration, viz. the date. In order to achieve this object the body of the stamp is perforated with four slots into which are fitted steel type, of which the small one uppermost bears an initial letter indicating the hour, whilst the other three serve to indicate respectively the day, month, and the year. The head of the stamp unscrews in such a manner as to afford ready access to the above-referred-to slots, so that the type may be changed as often as is requisite. The combination of the two stamps, i. e. the true obliterating stamp and its companion having been devised for a special purpose in England, it is questionable whether the same arrangement would be serviceable elsewhere. We are inclined to think that it would be better to employ but one stamp containing the name of the cancelling station and the date, as is shown in our sketch at the foot of Appendix D.

When the stamps are not used in the machine, they are fitted into a handle, as shown in the photographs above referred to. This handle, as will be seen, is provided with three holes in its head. The central hole is employed when only one stamp is used, as occasionally happens; the two outer ones are employed when two stamps are used in conjunction.

Reverting to the consideration of the

ink, we should state that although the primary
object of using fugitive ink is to render stamps
secure against being used more than once, another
most important advantage is gained by the use
of such ink, viz. the impossibility of reproducing
stamps printed therewith by the transfer process,
a method particularly applicable, as we have
shown, to stamps produced by the other systems.
The success of the transfer process of forgery
demands that the stamp to be copied should
be printed in an oleaginous ink, and since
the fugitive ink is not oleaginous it sets that
process at defiance, for the fugitive ink is not
subject to swell and become viscid when
steeped in dilute hydrochloric acid, nor will
it receive oil when applied to it in the manner
we have described in connection with stamps
printed by the other methods. Our fugitive
ink, in short, being entirely free from those
properties which render ordinary printing
ink so unfit for stamp printing, it follows
that stamps printed therewith by the most
perfect system (i. e. the surface) are undoubt
-edly as secure against forgery as it is possible
to render them, more especially as independently
of the impossibility of transferring them in the
manner we have discussed, the lithographic
process is not sufficiently refined to yield
prints that would in any way compare

21.

with surface printed stamps.

So far we have made reference exclusively to Postage Stamps. We will now, however, as briefly as possible explain the conditions which have to be fulfilled by Revenue, Customs, and Law Stamps. In the case of the former, the obliteration is always made by the Post Office officials, and it is, therefore, possible to enforce the use of a hand-stamp such as we have described; but with stamps which have to be used upon various documents, the case is different, as the duty of cancelling the stamp usually devolves upon the user thereof, and it would be unreasonable to expect that every individual called upon to affix a stamp to a document should be required to provide himself with a proper cancelling mark. Such stamps must almost of necessity, therefore, be cancelled by the simple process of writing across them. The ink in which they are printed has, consequently, to fulfil a totally different function to that in which the Postage Stamps are printed, which is fugitive only under the treatment of such liquids as could be employed for the removal of a printed cancellation; whereas in the case of the Revenue and like Stamps it is imperative to employ an ink which would be fugitive to such reagents as could be used for removing

22.

a written cancellation. Nevertheless, although such stamps are as a rule cancelled by writing, it is in some cases a matter of convenience to cancel them by a printed obliteration (in the Law Courts, for instance, where hand-stamps are always within reach). Consequently, in order to be fully protective, the ink in which such stamps are printed must be not only fugitive to reagents calculated to remove a written cancellation, but also to such as would remove a printed cancellation. This necessity has brought into use what we term " doubly fugitive" inks, such as we employ in the printing of Revenue, Customs and Law Stamps. We only have three "doubly fugitive" inks, specimens of which are given upon Appendix E. The doubly fugitive ink in which are printed the stamps at the head of this Appendix is generally employed for the lower duties of stamps, whilst the higher duties are by way of distinction printed in the green and the darker purple, like those in the specimens which follow. All three colours are, as we have said, "doubly fugitive", as will be seen by referring to our Appendix above referred to, wherein by the side of an uncancelled stamp we give in each case two specimens of cancelled stamps, one obliterated by writing and the other by printing.

23.

297

We have in each case treated that obliterated by writing with oxalic acid and that obliterated by printing with benzine. As will be seen, the former treatment destroys beyond restoration the colour of the stamp, whilst the latter treatment washes the body of the stamp away. In each case, the obliteration is much less disturbed than the stamp which it covers. Now, the Revenue, Customs and Law Stamps differ from the Postage Stamps only in this, that the former three are printed in our "doubly fugitive" inks, whilst the latter are printed in our "singly fugitive" inks. The conditions of security and of manufacture for both kinds of stamps are precisely the same, excepting that the former kinds are more difficult to print than the latter. This remark applies especially to the green and dark purple, as they are produced by a peculiar process which renders them exceedingly sensitive – so much so as to preclude their use where there is any chance of their being exposed to moisture or rough treatment of any kind, seeing that they are immediately destroyed by the action of water or by abrasion. When, therefore, Revenue, Customs, or Law Stamps are exposed to wear, the only colour available is the light purple in which are printed the stamps given at the head of our Appendix

24.

298

E. This colour, whilst possessing the peculiar "doubly fugitive" properties we have described, is as firm as the "singly fugitive" inks in which the Postage Stamps are printed.

Whilst we are upon the subject of Revenue Stamps, it is well to call attention to a peculiar form of such stamps which is employed by the Government of India. They find it expedient in the case of most legal instruments to enforce the use of what are termed "Stamped Papers," consisting of sheets of watermarked paper with elaborate stamps printed at their heads. Providing the instrument runs into more space than the "Stamped Paper" affords, it is continued upon ordinary paper cut down to the size of the "Stamped Paper" which forms its commencing page. Such "Stamped Papers" are to be highly recommended on account of the security which they afford. We give a specimen of one of the duties upon Appendix L, but in the case of India there are more than 100 duties, all of which are distinctive in device.

Having discussed in outline the various conditions and processes of adhesive stamp manufacture, it becomes important to show how the particular process in vogue is carried out, and what precautions are taken by the Governmental authorities in regard to control.

25.

We will, therefore, proceed to describe the course through which a ream of stamps (= 500 sheets) would go in its production.

The paper which is used contains a special watermark for each description of stamp, such watermark not only affording an additional protection as presenting an initial obstacle to the forger, but serving for purposes of control, seeing that stamps must be printed only upon the paper specially designed for them. The example at the top of Appendix I is a piece of watermarked stamp paper just as it came from the paper-making machine, being, however, only one of many descriptions of paper which we make for different kinds of stamps, the watermark varying in each description. The Dandyroll (the special apparatus employed in the pro-duction of the watermarks in the paper) are kept in a locked-up strong-room by Government officials, and are taken out by them only when a supply is required of the particular kind of paper for which a roll is applicable. An officer remains by the paper-making machine during the whole time that the paper is being made, and returns the dandyroll to the strong-room so soon as it is done with. We should mention that two officers are constantly employed in controlling the manufacture of our

26.

stamp papers, and that they keep the stock under lock
and key. Of this they serve out such quantities as
may be required from time to time, counting it carefully
sheet by sheet before parting with it. Each delivery
which they make is recorded in an account book.
Before the paper is handed over to us it undergoes
another process of counting, and after we have
satisfied ourselves by a third count that it is
correct in quantity, we hand a receipt to the
authorities for it, and pass it through the processes
necessary to prepare it for stamp printing.
Amongst them is the gumming process, by
which a quantity of gum is applied to the back
of the sheet sufficient to secure the adhesion of
the stamps to letters &c. The lower example in
Appendix F was cut from the same piece of
paper as the upper one, and after being subject
-ed to the process above referred to was highly
glazed. The paper having been brought
into this condition is taken to the printing
department, over which Government officers
preside. Before being received there, it is care-
-fully counted in order to make sure that the
right number of sheets are taken into the room
and an account of it is recorded in the proper
book. The printing process is carried on
under the immediate control of Government
Officers, who have in fact the entire charge
of the room, no less than the apparatus

employed therein, the principal part of which, such as the plates and dies they deposit in strong rooms (fire and thief-proof) for safety during the night as well as for Sundays and holidays. The fact of there being no fewer than 40 Government Officers in our Establishment superintending such work, and that the aggregate representative value of the Stamps which we produce annually, amounts to many million pounds will speak for itself as to the rigid system of control which prevails here, and will, we doubt not, ensure its appreciation.

We should explain that we carry on work for many Governments, each of which employs their own officers of control, so that we find it necessary to establish a separate printing department for each government. Supplying, as we do, the whole of the higher values of Stamps for the English Government, as well as the whole of those for that of India and the undermentioned Countries, it will be readily understood that the manufacture of stamps by us is one of a most extensive character.

Countries for which we manufacture stamps.

England   Antigua
India   Bahamas

28

Countries for which we manufacture Stamps
(continued)

Barbados	Nevis
Bermuda	St Christopher
British Guiana	St Helena
British Honduras	St Lucia
Cape of Good Hope	Sierra Leone
Ceylon	Straits Settlements
Dominica	Tasmania
Gambia	Trinidad
Gold Coast	Virgin Islands
Hong Kong	West Australia
Jamaica	Orange Free States
Lagos	New South Wales
Malta	South Australia
Mauritius	New Zealand
Montserrat	Victoria
Natal	

and many other foreign governments.

As we have stated above, the different Governments for whom we work have each a separate and distinct staff of officers for the purpose of supervision; nevertheless, the system of control which is adopted in each of our manufacturing Departments is similar to that which we have described above, and, as previously stated, the officers in charge have full control over all the apparatus

29.

and material engaged in the work, under their supervision, so that it becomes impossible for our workpeople, even if they were dishonestly disposed in any way to rob the Government whose work they are executing. The work is in fact as much under the control of the Governments concerned as if it were done in a Government office, we, however, being responsible for the proper conduct of the practical operations.

We will for the moment, with your permission, leave the subject of Adhesive Stamps to discuss a question which we think might be of interest to the Chinese Government. viz. that of Postage Envelopes. As you are aware, we manufacture a large quantity of such envelopes for the English home Government, as well as for that of India. In the latter country, they are found to be of great service, not only to the general public, but also to the Post Office officials, whose business is greatly facilitated by the use of proper covers for letters, instead of the insecure covers which were much in use by the natives of India before they were supplied by the Government with Postage Envelopes. They possess also this advantage that being of a uniform size and character they are much more easily dealt with than are letters covered by envelopes various as to

30.

size and shape. Circumstances may be different in China; nevertheless, we think that an appropriate form of Postage Envelope might be of great service there, seeing that even here in England it is found that the Postage Envelopes meet a real want, for to persons who are particular in such matters, an envelope with an embossed stamp has a better and neater appearance than one with an adhesive stamp affixed, to say nothing of the trouble saved (and that is the most important consideration) in affixing such stamps. In Appendix G., we give a specimen of one of the Postage Envelopes we make for the English Government, and in Appendix H. a specimen of the two kinds or duties which we make for India.   We reckon that the aggregate annual consumption of all these envelopes reaches no less than 58,000,000, a number which, moreover, is daily increasing. The Postage Stamp is embossed and printed with a coloured background in one operation by a somewhat elaborate machine.   The reason for the employment of the embossing process is that it is the only one which would give a really good result upon the envelopes at anything like a reasonable speed.   True it is that the same objections apply to the stamps under discussion as those

31.

we pointed out in connection with embossed adhesive Postage Stamps; at the same time a certain protection is undoubtedly given to them by the fact of their being impressed upon envelopes which there would be some difficulty in copying. It would be difficult for a forger to match the exact quality of our paper, or, even if he should do so he would be puzzled to make a perfectly successful imitation of the envelopes. Here, the envelope itself is in a measure secure from imitation; much more so when the Stamp has been impressed upon it. As a fact, although the kind of stamps employed are not so secure as could be wished, we have never received any serious complaints as to our Postage Envelopes being successfully imitated.

Now, we believe from what you have told us that the particular form of Envelope issued by the English and Indian Governments, as given in our Appendices G & H. would not serve the requirements of the Chinese public, but that such an envelope as that in Appendix I. would be more likely to be of service to them. More paper is wasted in cutting an envelope of this shape than in cutting one of the form of the English or Indian Postage Envelopes, but in other respects such an envelope would be almost as easily produced as they. The stamp

32.

could be affixed in the position we have indicated in any other place that might be desired. Underneath the envelopes in Appendix I, we have given drawings of two duties of embossed stamps which might be used upon them. It will be understood that the coloured parts represent the coloured background, whilst the white or shaded portions show those parts which would be raised in relief. We could produce such envelopes, of which we enclose 24, at about the rate of "11/- (eleven shillings) per thousand. This price would be exclusive of a charge of £65 (sixty five pounds) for the original embossing die and of £40 (forty pounds) for each duty die, but would include banding the envelopes in 24's with any printing on the band which might be required, packing them in tin-lined cases, and delivering them free on board ship in the London Docks.

It will of course be understood that we are in no way tied to the particular shape or size of our pattern envelope, but that we could at commensurate prices produce envelopes of any description that might be required both as to their form and the quality of paper employed besides being enabled to emboss them with stamps of any requisite device or duty.

Returning now to the Adhesive Postage Stamps, we beg to call your attention

33.

307

to our Appendix I, at the head of which you will find a design for what we should consider would be an appropriate watermark to employ in the paper for Chinese Stamps. This consists of the symbol Yin and Yang, deprived, however, of the nuclei, as those we could not render satisfactorily in the paper. Following the watermark design upon Appendix I, we give two sets or alternative designs for three different duties of chinese ethesive Postage Stamps. We have in each case adopted the same leading feature in the designs, that is to say the symbol Yin and Yang encircled by two dragons. Whilst, however, preserving this general characteristic, we have attempted to make the stamps as dissimilar as possible with the limited area at command, seeing that it is a matter of great importance that one value of stamp should be as strikingly unlike another as is practicable, not only to guard against the possibility of one duty being mistaken for another, but to render it impossible that by any manipulation a lower stamp should be converted into a higher one. For instance, supposing the 1 Candareen Stamp were the same in design and colour as the 2 Candareen stamp, the only difference between them being the Chinese characters denoting the duty, it is evident that the

34.

Chinese numeral 1 might be changed into a 2 and thus the 1 Candareen stamp be made to represent double its real value. That would be an instance of the simplest application of the particular mode of treatment in question, but it will be sufficient, we think, to show the desirability of making stamps unlike one another; and in fact experience has taught us that the more unlike they are in every way, the better. The designs which we have made are of the size of the English Postage Stamps, a size which it would be highly desirable to retain, seeing that all our apparatus is adapted for producing stamps of standard sizes (the one in question is the most appropriate for Postage Stamps) and that consequently any change as to size or shape would entail great expense.

The designs which we have been discussing are, of course, merely drawn by hand, and represent but very crudely the appearance which the finished stamps would present. We could throw a great amount of elaboration into the engraving of such designs, as will be at once apparent by referring to the specimen stamps given on Appendix A, or to the engraver's black proofs at the foot of Appendix I, from which it will be seen that we are enabled to bring our stamps to a high degree of refinement, and that anything

35.

of the nature of an animal is capable of treatment
quite as delicate as a head such as that adopted to
for the English Stamps. The symbol Yin and its
Yang combined with the dragons would give
considerable scope to our engravers; at the
same time we think that the effect of the finished
Stamps might be more pleasing were it possible
to adopt some kind of animal for a centre-piece
such as a tortoise, or any other creature typical
of China. This, however, would be a matter
entirely for the consideration of the Chinese
authorities. It will be understood that the
duties in the designs given upon Appendix
are merely suppositious, and that we should
have no difficulty in changing them for any
Chinese characters which might be required
further, that our designs could easily be modified
and that we should be able to make a distinctive
device for any number of duties which occasion
might call for.

　　　　　Supposing that we had to produce
Stamps after our designs, we should have to
make an original master die bearing the symbol
and the dragons; from that we should make
three other dies bearing the same symbol, and
upon the one which we might Select for the
One Candareen duty to engrave the remainder
of the work shown in the design. In like
manner one of the other two dies would be

36.

completed for the two Candareen and the third for
the five Candareen duty. If any additional dies
were at any time required, the requisite number
would be made from the master die, and the
appropriate completing patterns engraved on
them. By this system, we ensure the identity
of the leading feature of each die or stamp (a
great object as a matter of security), while
we avoid the trouble and expense of engraving
it upon each design, as would be the case
did we not avail ourselves of a peculiar method
which we cannot attempt to describe in the
compass of this letter, for reproducing the pattern
in the original master die upon those intended
to serve for the different duties.

So soon as the duty dies should have
been completed in the manner described, they
would furnish the means for producing the
plates. Our price for a master-die, would
be £75 (seventy five pounds); that for each duty
die £50 (fifty pounds); and that for each
printing plate of 240 multiples £85 (eighty
five pounds); whilst the dandyroll required to
produce the proposed watermark would cost
£80 (eighty pounds). Our price for the stamps
be £54. 3. 4 (fifty four pounds three shillings and
fourpence) per million. This price would
include packing them in tin-lined cases
and delivering them free on board ship in

[margin notes:]

Initial investment
master die £75
Dandyroll 80
Total £155

Special expense
which would have
to be entailed for
each duty of stamps
Duty die £50
Printing plate 85
total £135

37.

311

London. The price is for stamps gummed and perforated complete like the specimen quarter sheet of 12 Cents Hong Kong Postage Stamps given on Appendix K; and it is based upon the assumption that the stamps would be printed in sheets of 240 multiples, and that they would be subject to the like system of control as those we manufacture for the English, Indian or other Governments.

Regarding your request that we would give you some idea as to the cost of establishing Works in China for the production of Postage Stamps, we regret to say that it would be impossible for us to furnish even an approximate estimate of the expense which such a course would entail until we should know the probable number of stamps which would have to be produced per annum. At the same time, we may say that the cost of instituting such an establishment would be very heavy. Our feeling is, indeed, that it would be most unwise to attempt to carry out any such project until the Postage system had been given a fair trial, and until the production of the requisite stamps had been fully organized here in England; for even supposing that it were possible to establish Works in China competent to produce stamps of a satisfactory character, it is not for a moment to be supposed

38.

that it would be possible in such Works to provide for new requirements, seeing that independently of any other consideration our long experience in such matters would be found to be almost indispensable (we say so in all modesty). Added to this, it would be impossible without an inordinate expense to establish and maintain such a staff in China as would be competent to carry out the initiatory work, for which our arrangements are so complete. The course we should recommend would be that in the event of the Chinese Government deciding to employ us for the production of their Postage Stamps, they should, in case the quantities required were at first small, solicit the assistance of the Home Government, or that of India, in the control of their Stamp manufacture. If they should think it desirable, we should, of course, be quite willing that one or more representatives from their own country should be sent over to control the manufacture; but as in all probability the demands for stamps at the commencement would not be large, it appears to us that it would be better (in the first place at any rate) to try and utilize one or other of the controlling staffs which already exist, or failing that to employ some assistants from your own office for the purposes of control, seeing that

39.

by this means the Chinese Government would obtain absolutely the same security as if they employed their own officers of control. In the event of the consumption of stamps increasing, the Chinese Government could then if they pleased send their own representatives to take charge of the manufacture, and after the whole had been thoroughly organized and established here, it might become worth while for them to consider whether or not they would transfer the manufacture to their own country. We, however, incline to the belief that upon thorough investigation, the very difficult conditions of the work would decide them not to adopt such a course, seeing that even if our best workmen could be induced to go to China, they would not, we are sure, produce anything like the same quality of work that they do with us, for apart from the climatic difficulties + which would render the printing inks and other things concerned in the manufacture quite unmanageable which would undoubtedly occur, the lack of our personal supervision would inevitably tell very seriously against them. Independently of a reluctance on our part to assume a tone of self-laudation, we cannot here attempt to lay before you the very great difficulties inseparable from the stamp manufacture, such difficulties as are only to be overcome by the accumulated teachings of long experience added to very close personal attention on our part. That there exist such difficult conditions as we indicate,

40.

will, we think, be apparent to you from the considera-tion that amongst the thousands of printing estab--lishments which exist in England, ours is the only one in which such stamps as are under consideration are produced.

Should the Chinese Authorities decide upon employing us, and at the same time should they not approve of our designs, it would be well if they could have designs prepared for us to work to, and further if they would for each duty of stamp required send us all the characters which would have to appear upon the face thereof, written with clearness in black upon white paper or cardboard; moreover, it would be an advantage if such characters were to be written in duplicate or even in triplicate. Besides this, it would be well if an estimate could be formed of the probable annual consumption of each value of stamp or Postage Envelope. We would strongly recommend that the initial order should bespeak a stock sufficient to last for three years (i.e. one year's supply for use and two years' supply for stock,) seeing that in the case of India it is found necessary that a stock of two years' consumption should be always maintained there; otherwise there is a danger of its becoming exhausted before we can replenish it. This arises partly from the delay which takes place in the order reaching

4.

us; partly on account of the tedious processes through, which the stamps have to pass before completion; and partly from the time consumed, in their transit to India.

We trust you will not consider that we have allowed this letter to run to too great a length, but our wish to lay the matter before you in its principal bearings must be our apology for having entered into it so fully as we have done.

In conclusion, we beg to express our acknowledgments to the authorities concerned for their courtesy in supplying us with the specimens requisite to complete the Appendix to this letter, so important to the elucidation of the matter therein discussed.

We have the honour to be, Sir,
Your obedient servants,

42.

LONDON OFFICE OF THE INSPECTORATE GENERAL OF
CHINESE IMPERIAL MARITIME CUSTOMS:

8, STOREY'S GATE, St JAMES'S PARK, S.W.

21st June 1877

My dear Sir,

I have to thank you for your trade catalogue; and, I have no doubt, I shall have occasion (sooner or later) to apply to your firm for some of the supplies required by the authorities in China.

Yrs truly,

JD Campbell

W.M. de La Rue Esq.

[HOME FORM NO. 2.]

London Office of the Inspectorate-General of Chinese Maritime Customs.

INDENT No. _____   REQUISITION No. _____

TENDER _____

_____ hereby offer to supply (subject to inspection) of the best quality and

The shortest time make, free on board ship in _____, within *

that can be named from the date of order, the articles hereinafter specified, at the price set against each, making

with certainty together the sum of £ _____ *Abating all discounts or commissions*

Signature _____

Address _____

To THE SECRETARY,   Dated _____ this _____ day of _____ 18 ____
8, Storey's Gate, St. James's Park, S.W.

No.	DETAILED DESCRIPTION OF ARTICLE.	QUANTITY.	RATE NET CASH.	AMOUNT.	REMARKS.
1	Harrild Sons New Patent Treadle "Bremner" Platten Machines. Demy Folio. fitted with hand power. One extra ink-duct to be supplied with each Machine, and fitted so as to be readily changed	3.			
	Total cost of articles			£	
	Packing in best manner for shipment			£	
	Amount payable on receipt of Bill of Lading from Shipping Agents			£	

N.B.—Contractors are requested to be particular in filling up, dating and signing their Tenders.

[Home Form No. 2.] London Office of the Inspectorate-General of Chinese Maritime Customs.

INDENT No. _____　　　　　REQUISITION No. _____

TENDER _____

_____ hereby offer to supply (subject to inspection) of the best quality and

*The shortest time that can be named with certainty.

make, free on board ship in _____ , within* _____ from the date of order, the articles hereinafter specified, at the price set against each, making together the sum of £ _____ Abating all discounts or commissions

Signature _____

Address _____

To the Secretary,　　　　Dated _____ this _____ day of _____ 18___
8, Storey's Gate, St. James's Park, S.W.

No.	DETAILED DESCRIPTION OF ARTICLE.	QUANTITY.	RATE NET CASH.	AMOUNT.	REMARKS.
2.	Harrold Sons, Best quality Improved Round Hole Perforating Machines 25 in. wide. The above Perforating Machines are not to be supplied, if a Machine can be made to perforate more than one row at a time. A sheet of the exact size & design of the perforations to be made is enclosed	2			

Total cost of articles ... ... £

Packing in best manner for shipment ... ... £

Amount payable on receipt of Bill of Lading from Shipping Agents £

N.B.—Contractors are requested to be particular in filling up, dating and signing their Tenders.

中国海关总税务司署伦敦办事处订货单三

[Home Form No. 2.]

London Office of the Inspectorate-General of Chinese Maritime Customs.

INDENT Nº. _____   REQUISITION Nº. _____

TENDER _____

_____ hereby offer to supply (subject to inspection) of the best quality and

The shortest time make, free on board ship in _____ , within *X.*

that can be named from the date of order, the articles hereinafter specified, at the price set against each, making

with certainty together the sum of £ _____ *Abating all discounts or Commission*

Signature _____

Address _____

To the Secretary,   Dated _____ this _____ day of _____ 18___
8, Storey's Gate, St. James's Park, S.W.

Nº.	DETAILED DESCRIPTION OF ARTICLE.	QUANTITY.	RATE NET CASH.	AMOUNT.	REMARKS.
5	20 lbs. Lemon Yellow Ink. (Nº 3 in Specimen Book.)				
4	20 „ Mauve Ink. (Nº 15. Dº)				
3	20 „ Chocolate Ink (Nº 2. Dº)				
2	20 „ Crimson Lake Ink (Nº 13. Dº)				
1	20 „ Bright Green Ink (Nº 9 Dº)				
	10 „ Deep Orange Ink (Nº 5 Dº)				

Total cost of articles   ...   .   £

Packing in best manner for shipment   ...   ...   £

Amount payable on receipt of Bill of Lading from Shipping Agents   £

N.B.—Contractors are requested to be particular in filling up, dating and signing their Tenders.

323

中国海关总税务司署伦敦办事处订货单四

London Office of the Inspectorate-General of Chinese Maritime Customs.

INDENT No. _____   REQUISITION No. _____

TENDER _____

_____ hereby offer to supply (subject to inspection) of the best quality and

*The shortest time
that can be named
with certainty.*

make, free on board ship in _____ , within _____

from the date of order, the articles hereinafter specified, at the price set against each, making

together the sum of £ _____ *Abating all discounts or commission.*

Signature _____

Address _____

To THE SECRETARY,   Dated _____ this _____ day of _____ 18____
8, Storey's Gate, St. James's Park, S.W.

No.	DETAILED DESCRIPTION OF ARTICLE.	QUANTITY.	RATE NET CASH.	AMOUNT.	REMARKS.
	600 Reams of 500 Sheets each, of hand made paper, suitable for Postage Stamps, of the size & design of the accompanying sheet, with the water-mark of a rising sun on each square. The above paper must be forwarded as soon as possible, say 500 reams at a time can be ... for	600			

Total cost of articles	£		
Packing in best manner for shipment	£		
Amount payable on receipt of Bill of Lading from Shipping Agents	£		

N.B.—Contractors are requested to be particular in filling up, dating and signing their Tenders.

中国海关总税务司署伦敦办事处订货单五

[Home Form No. 2.]

London Office of the Inspectorate-General of Chinese Maritime Customs.

INDENT Nº. _____ REQUISITION Nº _____

TENDER _____

_____ hereby offer to supply (subject to inspection) of the best quality and

The shortest time make, free on board ship in _____ , within *·*
that can be named from the date of order, the articles hereinafter specified, at the price set against each, making
with certainty together the sum of £ _____ *Abating all discounts or Commission*

Signature _____

Address _____

To the Secretary,   Dated _____ this _____ day of _____ 18__
8, Storey's Gate, St. James's Park, S.W.

Nº.	DETAILED DESCRIPTION OF ARTICLE.	QUANTITY.	RATE NET CASH.	AMOUNT.	REMARKS.
	25 Gallons of specially prepared Gum or Composition for gumming Postage Stamps, a damp climate to be taken into consideration. The above composition must be supplied by monthly instalments of two gallons. If the ingredients can be obtained for mixing here it will be advisable to forward them dry	25			

Total cost of articles	£		
Packing in best manner for shipment	£		
Amount payable on receipt of Bill of Lading from Shipping Agents	£		

N.B.—Contractors are requested to be particular in filling up, dating and signing their Tenders.

中国海关总税务司署伦敦办事处订货单六

London Office of the Inspectorate-General of Chinese Maritime Customs.

INDENT N°. _____ REQUISITION N°.

TENDER _____

_____ hereby offer to supply (subject to inspection) of the best quality and

✕ *The shortest time* make, free on board ship in _____ , within ✕
that can be named from the date of order, the articles hereinafter specified, at the price set against each, making
with certainly together the sum of £ _____ *Abating all discounts or commission*

Signature _____

Address _____

To the Secretary, Dated_____ this_____ day of_____ 18
8, Storey's Gate, St. James's Park, S.W.

N°.	DETAILED DESCRIPTION OF ARTICLE.	QUANTITY.	RATE NET CASH.	AMOUNT.	REMARKS.
1	Letter Scales of the largest size the same as are used in the British Post Office.	20.			
2.	Letter Scales of the smallest size the same as are used in the British Post Office.	30.			
	Both sizes to be provided with Postal Union weights. (Grammes)				

				£
Total cost of articles	...	...	...	£
Packing in best manner for shipment	...	...	£
Amount payable on receipt of Bill of Lading from Shipping Agents	£

N.B.—Contractors are requested to be particular in filling up, dating and signing their Tenders.

In reply please refer to

№ 2475 S.

And address to the S.
SECRETARY
CHINESE CUSTOMS' OFFICE.

LONDON OFFICE OF THE INSPECTORATE GENERAL OF
CHINESE IMPERIAL MARITIME CUSTOMS:

8, STOREY'S GATE, ST JAMES'S PARK, S.W.

5ᵗʰ July 1877

Dear Sir,

Referring to our conversation of yesterday, I now enclose copy of the telegram I sent to the Inspector General.

The French Steamer, bringing the next mails from China has been wrecked and the mails have been lost. I fear that the promised memorandum, explanatory of the Requisitions already received and of those that

331

were to follow, may have been
despatched by this Steamer —
otherwise, it will no doubt be
forthcoming by the English Mail
due here on the 16ᵗʰ instant.

From the Requisitions, however,
which I have submitted to
your criticism, you may perhaps
be able to form some opinion
of the scale upon which
the Inspector General contemplates
commencing the production of
postage stamps in China, and
to estimate, accordingly, for the
machinery and appliances that
would be required there —
supposing that the Inspector

General prefers making the
stamps on the spot to having
them manufactured in England.
In this connection, it may
be necessary to consider which
of the several processes will
be the best adapted for the
climate and for the resources
possessed by the Customs'
printing Establishment at Shanghai.

I wish, however, to be
prepared to execute the order
with the utmost despatch, in
the event of the Inspector General
telegraphing back instructions to
supply the Stores in accordance
with the several Requisitions

that have been prepared in China.

I am, Dear Sir,

Yours truly

J.D. Campbell

W. W. de La Rue Esq.

Copy of telegram from Mr. Campbell to Mr. Hart, dated 4th July 1877.

"Postal Requisitions impracticable. Machine, Paper, Ink all unsuitable. Elaborate report mailed 22nd June. If you send immediately design for each stamp and, upon receipt report, telegraph instructions, all kinds can be ~~supplied~~ delivered here ten weeks afterwards, price £54 per Million. Special experience required. Time expense saved and protection from forgery ensured by starting manufacture here — transferring to China afterwards."

110 Bunhill Row, E.C.,
July 5th 1877.

Sir,

We should feel reluctant to tender for the machines and other things included in the Requisitions which you sent us upon the 2nd inst., seeing that in our view they are quite unsuitable for the purpose for which they are required, viz. for the manufacture of Postage Stamps. The "Bremner plates" is a very good machine for common type printing, but it is neither sufficiently powerful, nor in any way calculated to produce Stamps, and, in fact, it is really only adapted for the purpose for which it has been specially devised, viz. for "jobbing" printing.

We should not like to provide you with one of Messrs. Harrild's Perforating Machines, seeing that Messrs. Napier's machines although somewhat higher in price are, as our experience has taught us, infinitely superior to those of any other makers. At the same time, a treadle Perforating Machine is hardly suitable for perforating a large quantity of Stamps; for which it would be necessary, we think, to have the same form of machine as is employed by the Imperial Government at Somerset House.

J. D. Campbell Esq.
8 Storey's Gate, S.W.

337

The printing inks specified are those used for ordinary type printing, and are in no way suitable for stamp printing, seeing that when once such inks have become dry an obliteration can be removed from their surface without in any way destroying the print. Thus if stamps were printed in such inks, although they might be thoroughly obliterated they could very easily be cleaned and used a second time, without in any way revealing the fraud. It is, therefore, essential that stamps should be printed in none other than "fugitive" inks.

The hand-made paper about which enquiry is made would not be suitable for stamp printing, seeing that any paper which could be made by hand would be far too harsh for the reception of a fine print. When first we commenced the stamp manufacture, the paper-making machine had not been brought to anything like the perfection which has since been arrived at, and we had consequently at that time (we are speaking of 30 or 40 years ago) to employ hand-made paper for the stamps, but so soon as we could obtain a satisfactory water-mark in machine-made paper, we at once abandoned that made by hand, seeing that the printing upon it was always unsatisfactory and attended with great difficulties. Apart

2.

from this consideration, the fact that it is impossible
to ensure uniform thickness in hand-made paper
is another argument against its employment
for the particular purpose in question, for if the
paper vary in thickness the appearance of the
prints taken upon it will also vary, seeing that
if thinner or thicker paper than that for which
the press is adjusted be used either the impression
will be too light or too heavy, thus imparting a
very different appearance to the stamps. Now,
it is important that stamps should not only be
inherently good but uniform in appearance, so
that the users thereof may be able to recognize
a genuine stamp without hesitation.

The paper should be prepared on one
side and then gummed before printing, so that
it would not be necessary to supply any gum
or composition, but we fear that if an attempt
were made to send out gummed paper to China
it might possibly be injuriously affected by
moisture, even though it were packed in tin-
lined cases.

As you will gather by the above
remarks, we are of opinion that the machinery
and appliances which have been indented for
are altogether unfit for the purpose for which
they are required. We fully appreciate, however,
the difficulty which must have been experienced by the framer of the Requisition (in

5.

consequence of his being unfamiliar with the special conditions to be fulfilled) in the selection of such things as might appear necessary, for the production of stamps, and we think that under the circumstances he could not well have made a better choice

We are in hopes that the Chinese Government will decide to avail themselves of our experience in the Postage Stamp manufacture, for it appears to us to be of the very first importance that the stamps which they employ, should be of such a nature as to inspire confidence, seeing that should they be insecure it would inevitably result that they would be freely forged in China, and that consequently the whole system of collecting revenue by means of stamps would be discredited, whereas if stamps were issued such as would be secure against forgery, there is every probability that the system would extend beyond that of the postal service, and that in time a vast revenue would be collected through the agency of stamps as is the case in India. That these conclusions are well founded is shown by what has taken place in the latter country. When some thirty years ago, we were first applied to by the Government of India to manufacture stamps, their use was practically limited to the postage service; but since

4.

that time we have been employed for the production of a great variety of Indian Stamps, by means of which very large revenues are collected annually, and there is no doubt whatever that the reason for the extension of the system is that confidence is felt in the security of the stamps, and that if such confidence were lacking their use would have been limited almost to what it was formerly. We refer to India more particularly because it appears to us that the conditions there and in China are somewhat similar, seeing that the natives of both countries are renowned for their patience and skill as copyists but the same arguments would apply in the case of England and many other countries which we have supplied with stamps, excepting that in a more highly civilized land there would appear to be other checks for the protection of the Government, besides the actual security of the stamps. That is not, however, any reason why secure stamps should not be employed and the English Government has always found it advantageous to obtain from us those of the highest character. These considerations, and those into which we entered so fully in our letter of the 18th ulto. will, we have no doubt, convince the authorities concerned in initiating the

5.

Postal System in China of the advantage to be derived from employing for their purpose stamps of the highest class which can be obtained, viz. those produced by our improved system.

We have the honour to be, Sir,
Your obedt. servants,

1877 年 7 月 6 日金登干致德纳罗函

No. 2483.

LONDON OFFICE OF THE INSPECTORATE GENERAL OF

CHINESE MARITIME CUSTOMS:

8, Storey's Gate, St. James's Park; S.W.

6th July 1877.

Gentlemen,

I beg to acknowledge the receipt of your letter of yesterday's date and to thank you for the observations, you have been so good as to favour me with, upon the Postal Requisitions referred to you on the 2nd instant.

I am quite of your opinion that gummed paper would be injuriously affected by moisture, during transport to China; and I would enquire, therefore, whether it would

Messrs. De la Rue & Co.
Bunhill Row,
E. C.

343

would not be possible to make the gum composition on the spot, if the necessary materials were sent out.

I shall be glad to hear from Mr. W. W. De La Rue. (in reply to the letter I addressed him yesterday) whether, taking into consideration the circumstances under which the Requisitions were prepared in China, he could suggest any way of meeting the requirements and enabling the Customs' printing establishment at Shanghai to commence the production of postage stamps on the 1st of October next.

I am,

Gentlemen,

Your obedient Servant,

J. D. Campbell

July 6. 1877.

My dear Sir,

I am much obliged to you for your letter of yesterday, and for the copy of the telegram which it enclosed. I infer from what you say that you propose to await an answer to this telegram before taking any action in the matter, and this would certainly seem the best course. So soon as you receive a further communication

J. D. Campbell Esq.

from China, I shall be glad to see you upon the subject; for if, notwithstanding all the arguments against such a course the Inspector General decides to print the stamps in China he must of course be furnished with the proper means of doing so, & we should be happy to lend you every assistance in the matter. I am in hopes, however, that he will decide to have the manufacture at least initiated by us.

You will no doubt have received our formal letter of today.

Yrs. very truly

P. T. O.

P. S. Your letter of this morning is just to hand, and we should of course have to try and make some gumming composition which could be sent to China, should it be decided to manufacture the stamps there, but even in this case the paper would have to have a coat of preparation before it was sent.

As I have said above, if, after all, it is decided that the stamps must be manufactured in China, we should be happy to assist you as far as possible, but we hope that the Inspector-General will come to a wiser Conclusion. I suppose, however, nothing can be done until you receive a telegram from China, or do you think any of the matters — such as the dies and printing plates — might be put in hand at once.

In compliance with the request conveyed through your messenger, I return you the diagram which accompanied your Requisition forms.

1877 年 12 月 17 日金登干致德纳罗函

24

INDENT No. *193*.

[To be quoted on all Letters and Documents relating to this order.]

RECEIVED
18 DEC 77
FOR
THOS DE LA RUE & CO

London Office of the Inspectorate-General of Chinese Maritime Customs;

8, Storey's Gate, St. James's Park, S.W.;

17th Dec* 1877.

Gentlemen,

You are invited to forward to this Office, as soon as possible, a Tender on the enclosed Form for the articles *in Duplicate* specified therein.

Tender in Duplicate.

Should you not be inclined to contract for the same, you are requested to be good enough to return the Form *in Duplicate* to this Office at your earliest convenience.

I am,

Your obedient Servant,

J.D. Campbell

Secretary.

To

Messrs De La Rue & Co.
Bunhill Row,
E. C.

349

1877 年 12 月 19 日德纳罗标书

CHINESE IMPERIAL MARITIME CUSTOMS.

INDENT N⁰. 166.   *Shanghai*   REQUISITION N⁰. 19.

Duplicate.

TENDER *for Cloth boards for binding books,*

We hereby offer to supply (subject to inspection) of the best quality and make, free on board ship in *London*, within* *Seven weeks* from the date of order, the articles hereinafter specified, at the price set against each, making together the sum of £ *56 n 3 n 4* net cash.†

N.B.—The shortest time that can be stated with certainty.

Signature *Norlet Ri....... Co*

Address *110 Bunhill Row, London, EC*

†N.B.—The Tender should show the net sum payable after deduction of any usual trade discount: no commission is to be paid or allowed by the Contractor to any person on any account whatever.

To THE SECRETARY,
Chinese Customs Office,
8, Storey's Gate, St. James's Park, S.W.

Dated _____ this *19th* day of *December* 18 *77*.

N⁰.	DETAILED DESCRIPTION OF ARTICLE.	QUANTITY.	RATE. NET CASH.	AMOUNT.	REMARKS.
	One thousand dark green cloth boards, to contain 37 sheets (folded in quarto) of the toned demy of which specimen is enclosed. The outside of front cover to bear a stamp in gilt, in facsimile of the Chinese characters at the head of the title page enclosed, the back to be lettered *Le Saint Edit.* *A. F. Pous.* Shanghai. Bureau des Statistiques Douanes Impériales — The				Both sides to have a handsome blind border and the first side the Chinese letters in gold in addition. The back to be worked in gold & blind. See over
	Carried forward				

351

N°.	DETAILED DESCRIPTION OF ARTICLE.	QUANTITY.	RATE. NET CASH.	AMOUNT.	REMARK
	Brought forward ...				
	The sides to be stamped with some neat & appropriate design for a border.				
	N.B. These covers are wanted in China at the earliest possible date.	1000	1/1	54 3 4	

Nᵒ.	DETAILED DESCRIPTION OF ARTICLE.	QUANTITY.	RATE. NET CASH.	AMOUNT.	REMARKS.
	Brought forward				

Total cost of articles	£	54	3	4	
Packing **in best manner** for shipment ...	£	2			
Net Amount, payable on Receipt of Bills of Lading from Shipping Agents.	£	56	3	4	

N.B.—Contractors are requested to be particular in filling up, dating, and signing their Tenders.

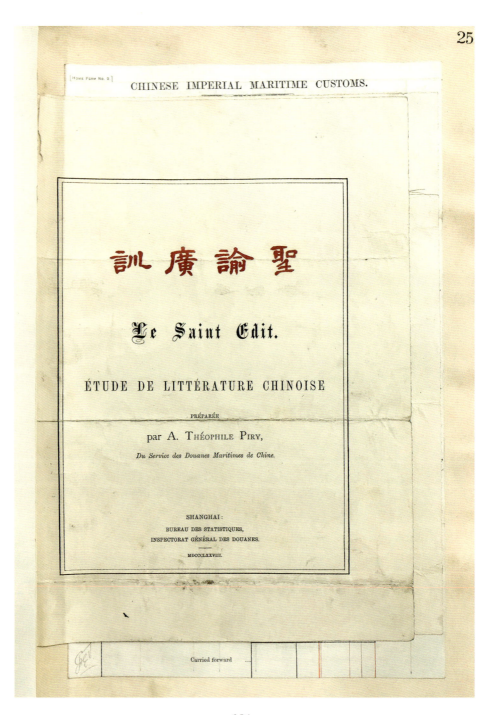

[Home Form No. 2.]

CHINESE IMPERIAL MARITIME CUSTOMS.

聖諭廣訓

Le Saint Edit.

ÉTUDE DE LITTÉRATURE CHINOISE

PRÉPARÉE

par A. Théophile Piry,

Du Service des Douanes Maritimes de Chine.

SHANGHAI:

BUREAU DES STATISTIQUES,

INSPECTORAT GÉNÉRAL DES DOUANES.

MDCCCLXXVIII.

Carried forward ...

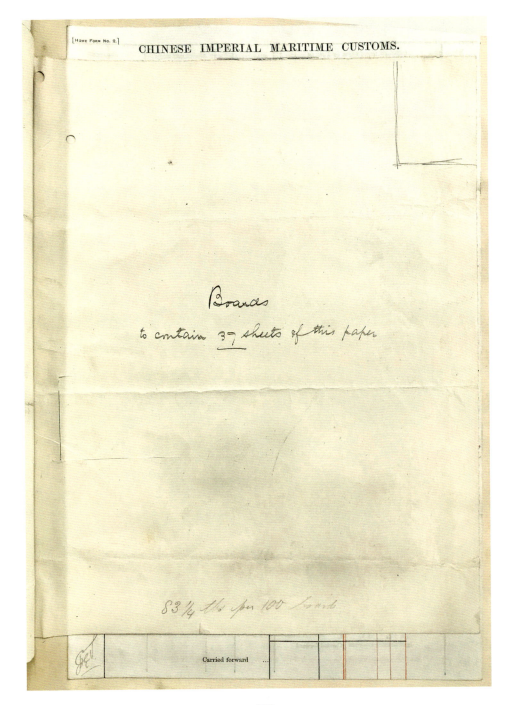

1877 年 12 月 21 日订货函

Order
INDENT Nº 193

[To be quoted on all Letters and
Documents relating to this Order.]

London Office of the Inspectorate-General of

Chinese Maritime Customs;

8, Storey's Gate, St. James's Park; S.W.,

21st December 1877

Gentlemen,

I have to request that you will supply the

1000 dark green cloth boards

in accordance with your tender of the 19th instant.

I will thank you to acknowledge the receipt

of this letter and to notify me when the stores are ready for

inspection.

I am,

Gentlemen,

Your obedient Servant,

F. E. Taylor

pro Secretary.

To
Messrs.
Thos: De La Rue & Co:
10 Bunhill Row.
E.C.

357

1877 年 12 月 22 日德纳罗致金登干函

December 22nd 7.

Sir,

We have to thank you for your letter of yesterday, accepting our Tender of the 19th inst. for the supply of 1,000 dark green Cloth Boards. This order shall have our immediate attention.

We understand that you require us to send in a duplicate of our Tender, but as we thought that the duplicate form you furnished us with was intended for our own use we have fastened it in a book. This being the case, we should feel much obliged if you would kindly send us another form, which we will duly fill in and return

J. D. Campbell Esq.,
8 Storey's Gate,
St. James's Park.

359

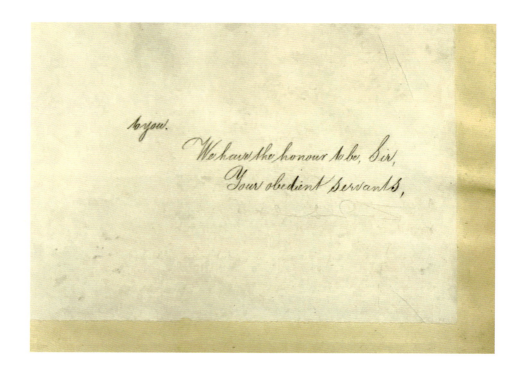

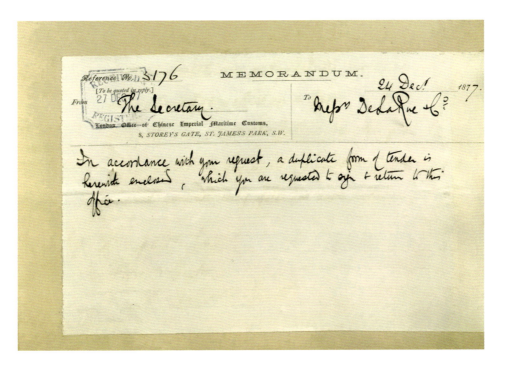

Reference No. 3176   MEMORANDUM.

[To be quoted in reply.]

From The Secretary.

London Office of Chinese Imperial Maritime Customs,
8, STOREY'S GATE, ST. JAMES'S PARK, S.W.

24 Dec.ʳ 1877.

To Mesrˢ DeLaRue & Co.

In accordance with your request, a duplicate form of tender is herewith enclosed, which you are requested to sign & return to this office.

1878 年 1 月 22 日海关伦敦办事处函

L. O. Form No. 9.

ORDER No. 193

For Cloth Board Covers.

London Office of the Inspectorate General of Chinese Maritime Customs,

8, STOREY'S GATE, ST. JAMES'S PARK, S.W.

22 January 1878.

Gentlemen,

1. With reference to the Stores supplied by you under Order No. 193, you are requested to have the cases, &c., marked in accordance with the printed directions enclosed, and numbered from No. 1 upwards.

1. Marking Instructions

2. Shipping Instructions will be sent to you, upon your returning to this office, properly filled up in duplicate, the enclosed Schedules of Packages, showing the Nos., description, weight, measurement, value, &c., of each Case or Package in detail, for the purposes of shipment and insurance.

2. Schedule of Packages in duplicate

3. You are also requested to return, as soon as possible, the enclosed Packing Accounts, properly filled up in duplicate, showing the contents of each Case or Package in detail; and to forward, at the same time, your monied Invoices in triplicate, the items being entered therein in the same order in which they are stated in your Tender. Payment of the same will be made upon receipt of the Bills of Lading from the Shipping Agent.

3. Packing Accounts in Triplicate

I am,

Gentlemen,

Your obedient Servant,

J. D. CAMPBELL,

Secretary.

Entered Export Day Book

To Messrs. Thos. De La Rue & Co. Folio A

110 Bunhill Row. E.C.

363

London Office of the Inspectorate General of Chinese Maritime Customs.

DIRECTIONS FOR MARKING CASES, &c.

The Cases should be marked in accordance with this Diagram— bearing the distinctive mark of the Chinese Imperial Maritime Customs on the top of each case, the destination on the front, and a general description of the contents on the left side, for the guidance of the authorities in China.

Casks and all other Pieces and Packages *should be similarly marked as far as possible, and where the nature of the Package will not allow of its being marked, Labels, properly addressed as above, should be securely fastened to it as shown in the following drawing of a Coil of Wire.*

The Label is placed inside the Coil to protect the address from abrasion.

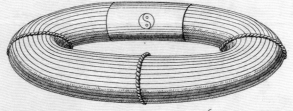

NOTE.—The Mark is constructed by describing two equal semi-circles with a circle round them, thus:— the right side of the figure is dark, having the centre or eye of the upper semi-circle bright, whilst the left side is bright and the eye dark.

附录　大龙邮品集萃

赫德画稿

源流：

罗伯特·赫德爵士（Sir Robert Hart）

约翰·A. 阿格纽（John A. Agnew）

珀西瓦尔·大卫德爵士（Sir Percival David）

水原明窗（Meiso Mizuhara）

（图片提供：北京保利国际拍卖有限公司）

设计图稿（云龙图、宝塔图、大象图）

源流：

罗伯特·赫德爵士（Sir Robert Hart）

约翰·A.阿格纽（John A. Agnew）

珀西瓦尔·大卫德爵士（Sir Percival David）

水原明窗（Meiso Mizuhara）

（图片提供：Spink China）

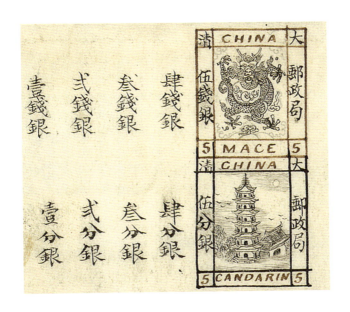

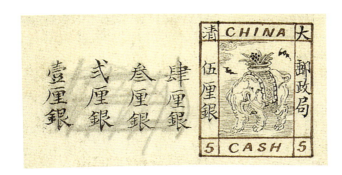

试样（云龙图、宝塔图、大象图）

云龙图源流：

罗伯特·赫德爵士（Sir Robert Hart）

约翰·A. 阿格纽（John A. Agnew）

珀西瓦尔·大卫德爵士（Sir Percival David）

理查德·卡门（Richard Canman）

水原明窗（Meiso Mizuhara）

宝塔图、大象图源流：

罗伯特·赫德爵士（Sir Robert Hart）

约翰·A. 阿格纽（John A. Agnew）

珀西瓦尔·大卫德爵士（Sir Percival David）

水原明窗（Meiso Mizuhara）

（图片提供：Spink China）

大象图（亦称"万年有象"图）母模印样

源流：

杰拉尔德·吉尔伯特（Gerard Gilbert）

郭植芳（Allen Gokson）

邹启祥（C.S. Tsou）

里昂·F. 利文斯顿（Lyons F. Livingston）

水原明窗（Meiso Mizuhara）

（图片提供：Spink China）

大象图无齿全张印样

大卫德爵士（Sir Percival David）曾收藏一件无齿大象图横五连，源自赫德爵士（Sir Robert Hart）和阿格纽（John A. Agnew）。周今觉先生在《邮乘》（第一卷第一号）著文称其亦收藏一件横五连，源自英国邮商，为横十连分拆。美国集邮家勒夫（John N. Luff）谓曾见过一件100 枚的全张，艾尔兰（Philip. W. Ireland）也认为至少有一个全张存世。2010 年 9 月，孙吉博士（Dr. Sun Ji）在《中国飞剪》（*The China Clipper*）第 74 卷第 6 期发表文章，首次公开了大象图无齿全张印样。

（图片提供：孙吉博士）

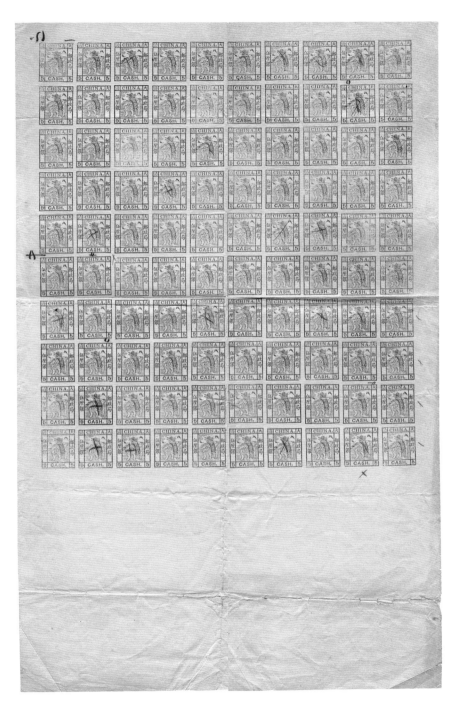

大象图有齿二十五方连

源流：

约翰·N. 勒夫（John. N. Luff）

詹姆斯·施塔上校（Major James Starr）

陈拓雄（Chen Tuoh Hsiung）

（图片提供：陈拓雄先生）

大龙邮票一分银母模印样

源流：

约翰·N. 勒夫（John N. Luff）

E.H. 费纳根（E.H. Finegan）

珀西瓦尔·大卫德爵士（Sir Percival David）

理查德·卡门（Richard Canman）

水原明窗（Meiso Mizuhara）

（图片提供：Spink China）

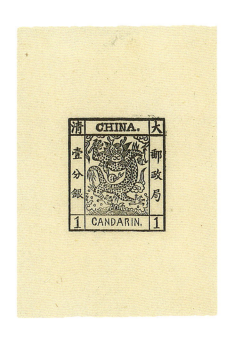

大龙邮票一分银试模印样（多一圈）

源流：

詹姆斯·施塔上校（Major James Starr）

贝克曼夫妇（Anna-Lisa and Sven-Eric Beckeman）

（图片提供：Sotheby's and Corinphila）

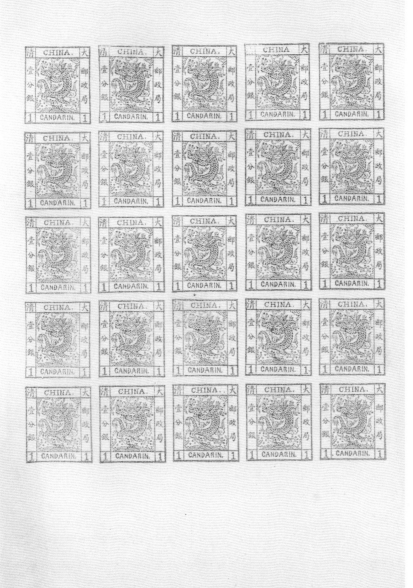

大龙邮票三分银试模印样（多一圈）

源流：

詹姆斯·施塔上校（Major James Starr）

林文琰（Lam Man Yin）

（图片提供：Interasia Auctions）

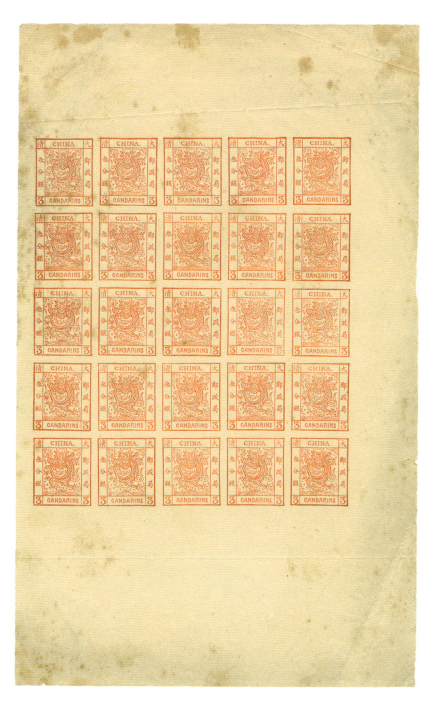

大龙邮票五分银试模印样（多一圈）

源流：

菲利普·W. 艾尔兰（Philip W. Ireland）

贝克曼夫妇（Anna-Lisa and Sven-Eric Beckeman）

（图片提供：Sotheby's and Corinphila）

大龙邮票五分银试模印样（多一圈，有齿）

源流：

罗伯特·赫德爵士（Sir Robert Hart）

珀西瓦尔·大卫德爵士（Sir Percival David）

朱利奥·莫基（Giulio Mochi）

贝克曼夫妇（Anna-Lisa and Sven-Eric Beckeman）

（图片提供：Sotheby's and Corinphila）

大龙邮票一分银试版印样

源流：

贝克曼夫妇（Anna-Lisa and Sven-Eric Beckeman）

（图片提供：Sotheby's and Corinphila）

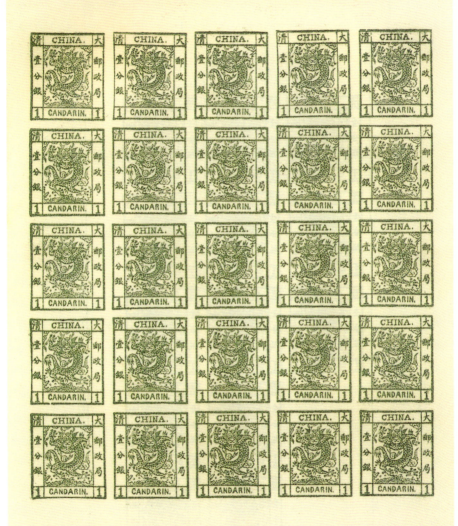

大龙邮票三分银试版印样

源流：

贝克曼夫妇（Anna-Lisa and Sven-Eric Beckeman）

（图片提供：Sotheby's and Corinphila）

大龙邮票五分银试版印样

源流：

戈佛雷·梅勒（Godfrey Mellor）

保罗·霍克（Paul Hock）

菲利普·W. 艾尔兰（Philip. W. Ireland）

奥尔森夫妇（Jane and Dan Sten Olsson）

（图片提供：Interasia Auctions）

大龙邮票五分银试色印样

源流：

大卫德爵士（Sir Percival David）

朱利奥·莫基（Giulio Mochi）

贝克曼夫妇（Anna-Lisa and Sven-Eric Beckeman）

（图片提供：Interasia Auctions）

大龙邮票薄纸一分银全张

（图片提供：Interasia Auctions）

大龙邮票薄纸三分银全张

（图片提供：Interasia Auctions）

大龙邮票薄纸五分银全张

（图片提供：Interasia Auctions）

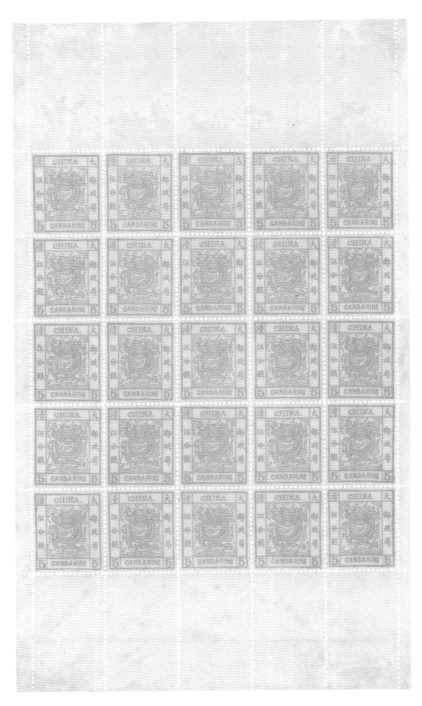

大龙邮票阔边一分银全张

源流：

沃伦·G. 高达医生（Dr. Warren G. Kauder）

贝克曼夫妇（Anna-Lisa and Sven-Eric Beckeman）

（图片提供：Spink China）

大龙邮票阔边五分银全张

源流：

詹姆斯·施塔上校（Major James Starr）

林文琰（Lam Man Yin）

丁劲松（Ding Jin Song）

（图片提供：丁劲松先生）

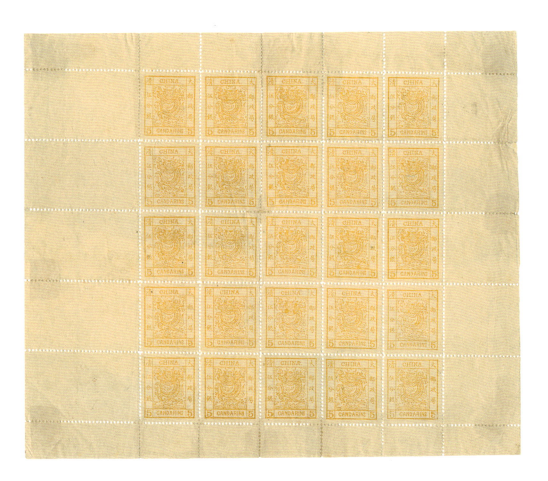

大龙邮票厚纸一分银全张

源流：

乔治·沃辛顿（George Worthington）

E.H. 费纳根（E.H. Finegan）

珀西瓦尔·大卫德爵士（Sir Percival David）

保罗·霍克（Paul Hock）

菲利普·W. 艾尔兰（Philip W. Ireland）

贝克曼夫妇（Anna-Lisa and Sven-Eric Beckeman）

陈拓雄（Chen Tuoh Hsiung）

（图片提供：陈拓雄先生）

大龙邮票厚纸三分银全张

源流：

贝克曼夫妇（Anna-Lisa and Sven-Eric Beckeman）

陈拓雄（Chen Tuoh Hsiung）

（图片提供：陈拓雄先生）

大龙邮票厚纸五分银全张

源流：

贝克曼夫妇（Anna-Lisa and Sven-Eric Beckeman）

陈拓雄（Chen Tuoh Hsiung）

（图片提供：陈拓雄先生）

1878 年 10 月 5 日北京寄上海封

1878 年 10 月 5 日，北京寄上海。

正面：贴大龙薄纸伍分银横双连及单枚，销 1878 年 10 月 5 日蓝色北京海关总税务司署日戳。10 月 12 日到达上海，销红色上海海关日戳。左下角加盖紫色秘鲁公使馆椭圆印。

背面：销蓝色 1878 年 10 月 12 日蓝色上海工部书信馆日戳。封口钤红色秘鲁公使馆火漆印。

已知存世最早的大龙邮票实寄封，号称"华邮第一古封"。

源流：陈海忠（H.C. Chen）、王振家（T.C. Wong）、陈志川（T.C. Chen）、郭植芳（Allen Gokson）、沃伦·G. 高达医生（Dr. Warren G. Kauder）、黄天湧（James Huangco）、庄顺成（Cheng Sun-Sing）、黄建斌（James B. Whang）、贝克曼夫妇（Anna-Lisa and Sven-Eric Beckeman）、奥尔森夫妇（Jane and Dan Sten Olsson）

（图片提供：Interasia Auctions）

414

1878 年 10 月 7 日北京寄上海封

1878 年 10 月 7 日，北京寄上海。

正面：贴大龙薄纸伍分银双连，销盖 1878 年 10 月 7 日蓝色北京海关总税务司署日戳。1878 年
10 月 12 日到达上海，销红色上海海关日戳，左下角加盖紫色秘鲁公使馆椭圆印。

背面：销 1878 年 10 月 12 日蓝色上海工部书信馆日戳。封口钤红色秘鲁公使馆火漆印。

此件信函比前页 10 月 5 日的信函晚两天收寄，但同一天（10 月 12 日）到达上海。

源流：索尔·纽伯里（Saul Newbury）、迈克尔·纽伯里（Michael Newbury）、沃伦·G. 高达
医生（Dr. Warren G. Kauder）、朱利奥·莫基（Giulio Mochi）、林文琰（Lam Man Yin）、丁劲松
（Ding Jin Song）

（图片提供：丁劲松先生）

416

1878 年 11 月 23 日北京寄上海封

1878 年 11 月 23 日，北京寄上海。

正面：贴大龙薄纸伍分银单枚，销盖蓝色北京"PAID"长条戳，左下角加盖紫色秘鲁公使馆椭圆印。

背面：销 1878 年 11 月 23 日蓝色北京海关总税务司署日戳、1878 年 11 月 29 日红色上海海关日戳和同日蓝色上海工部书信馆日戳。背面封口加盖紫色秘鲁公使馆椭圆印。

唯一用"PIAD"戳销盖邮票的大龙实寄封。

源流：朱利奥・莫基（Giulio Mochi）、林文琰（Lam Man Yin）、丁劲松（Ding Jin Song）

（图片提供：丁劲松先生）

1878 年 12 月 20 日美国寄上海封

1878 年 12 月 20 日，美国沃伦（Warren）寄上海。

正面：贴 5 分美国邮票，销盖环靶形戳和 12 月 20 日沃伦日戳。1879 年 2 月 6 日到达上海，贴大龙薄纸壹分银两枚、叁分银一枚，销 1879 年 2 月 6 日红色上海海关戳。

已知最早的贴大龙邮票进口实寄封。

源流：沃伦·G. 阿特伍德（Dr. Warren G. Atwood）、水原明窗（Meiso Mizuhara）

（图片提供：Spink China）

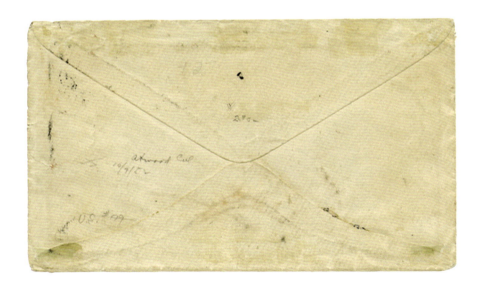

1879 年 5 月 26 日镇江寄英国明信片

1879 年 5 月 26 日，镇江寄英国圣安德鲁斯（St. Andrews）。

正面：贴大龙薄纸叁分银单枚，销盖 1879 年 5 月 26 日镇江海关戳。5 月 27 日上海转口，销上海海关戳和英国客邮局"A"号戳，格式明信片所贴 5 分香港邮票销盖英国上海客邮局"S1"杀手戳。7 月 14 日到达圣安德鲁斯，销"A"号日戳。

背面：5 月 31 日香港中转，销香港"C"号日戳。

已知最早加贴大龙邮票的明信片。

源流：朱利奥·莫基（Giulio Mochi）、水原明窗（Meiso Mizuhara）、丁劲松（Ding Jin Song）

（图片提供：丁劲松先生）

1879 年 10 月 8 日英国寄上海封

1879 年 10 月 8 日，英国贝尔法斯特（Belfast）寄上海。

正面：贴英国 4 便士和 2 便士邮票各一枚，销盖 1879 年 10 月 8 日贝尔法斯特"15"号日戳和"62"号杀手戳。左下角加贴大龙薄纸叁分银一枚，销盖上海海关"C.P.D."条形戳。

背面：销 10 月 8 日 Bancor "C"号日戳，11 月 17 香港中转，销"A"号日戳，11 月 22 日到达上海，销上海海关日戳。

唯一用"C.P.D."条形戳销盖大龙邮票的实寄封。

源流：彼得·霍尔康（Peter Holcome）、林文琰（Lam Man Yin）、丁劲松（Ding Jin Song）

（图片提供：丁劲松先生）

1882 年 10 月 26 日上海本埠封

1882 年 10 月 26 日，上海本埠邮件。

正面：贴大龙阔边叁分银和工部小龙二十文邮票各一枚，工部小龙销盖 1882 年 10 月 26 日蓝色上海工部书信馆日戳，大龙邮票销盖 1882 年 10 月 26 日红色上海海关日戳。

背面：销 1882 年 10 月 26 日蓝色上海工部书信馆日戳和红色上海海关日戳。

唯一的大龙邮票和工部书信馆邮票混贴封。

源流：珀西瓦尔·大卫德爵士（Sir Percival David）、吴乐园（L.Y. Woo）、黄兼慈（Joseph K.C. Wong）、黄建斌（James B. Whang）、林文琰（Lam Man Yin）、丁劲松（Ding Jin Song）

（图片提供：丁劲松先生）

1882 年 12 月 8 日英国寄牛庄封

1882 年 12 月 8 日，英国曼彻斯特（Manchester）寄牛庄封。

正面：贴英国 1 便士和 4 便士邮票各一枚，销盖"498"号杀手戳和 1882 年 12 月 8 日曼彻斯特黑色日戳。另销 1883 年 2 月 17 日牛庄海关日戳和"TO PAY"长方戳。

背面：贴大龙薄纸壹分银横三连，销盖 1883 年 2 月 17 日牛庄海关日戳。另销 1883 年 1 月 15 日香港"B"号日戳、1883 年 1 月 21 日上海英国客邮局"A"号戳和 1883 年 1 月 22 日红色上海海关戳。

唯一加盖"TO PAY"的大龙邮票进口封。

源流：索尔·纽伯里（Saul Newbury）、迈克尔·纽伯里（Michael Newbury）、高七来（C.L. Kao）、石用良井（Ryohei Ishikawa）、贝克曼夫妇（Anna-Lisa and Sven-Eric Beckeman）、奥尔森夫妇（Jane and Dan Sten Olsson）

（图片提供：Interasia Auctions）

1882 年 12 月 22 日天津寄北京封

1882 年 12 月 23 日，天津寄北京。

正面：注明封信时间：光绪捌年拾一月拾叁日戌时正二刻（1882 年 12 月 22 日晚 7 点半）。

背面：贴大龙阔边叁分银直双连，销天津 2 型篆字海关中文戳。另销 1882 年 12 月 23 日天津海关戳和天津海关拨驲达书信馆（光绪）八年十一月十四日（1882 年 12 月 23 日）方形戳。

源流：李纪润（C.J. Li）、郭植芳（Allen Gokson）、陈志川（T.C. Chen）、邵洵美（H.M. Shao）、郭植芳、彼得·霍尔康（Peter Holcome）、林文琰（Lam Man Yin）、丁劲松（Ding Jin Song）

（图片提供：丁劲松先生）

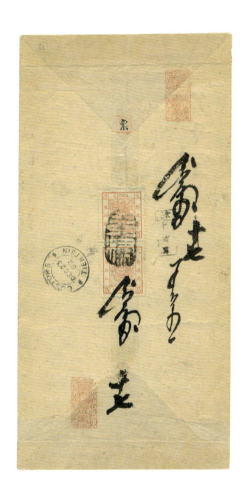

第四拾號泥局來報錄封交津海關稅務司由撥駟達遞呈

總理各國事務衙門鈞票

光緒捌年拾壹月拾叁日戌時二刻　分天津電報總局謹封

1883 年 3 月 25 日北京寄德国封

1883 年 3 月 25 日，北京寄德国慕尼黑（Munchen）。

正面：贴法国客邮 25 生丁和 1 法郎各一枚，销盖 1883 年 4 月 4 日上海法国客邮局日戳，另销 1883 年 4 月 8 日法国轮船邮局日戳。

背面：贴大龙阔边伍分银凹字形九方连，销盖北京蓝色椭圆中文海关戳。另销 1883 年 3 月 25 日蓝色北京海关总税务司署日戳、1883 年 3 月 30 日上海海关日戳和 1883 年 5 月 12 日慕尼黑日戳。

已知贴用大龙阔边伍分银邮票最多的实寄封。

源流：沃伦·G. 高达医生（Dr. Warren G. Kauder）、朱利奥·莫基（Giulio Mochi）、贝克曼夫妇（Anna-Lisa and Sven-Eric Beckeman）、大卫·富门（David Feldman）

（图片提供：Spink China）

1883 年 11 月 29 日北京寄意大利封

1883 年 11 月 29 日，北京寄意大利罗马（Rome）。

正面：贴法国客邮 75 生丁一枚和 1 法郎横三连，销盖 1883 年 12 月 5 日上海法国客邮局日戳。

背面：贴大龙薄纸叁分银五方连和大龙厚纸伍分银二十四方连，销盖蓝色椭圆北京中文海关戳。

另销 1883 年 11 月 29 日蓝色北京海关总税务司署日戳、1883 年 12 月 4 日蓝色上海海关日戳和 1884 年 1 月 17 日罗马日戳。封口贴有红色北京德国公使馆封签。

已知贴用大龙邮票最多的实寄封。

源流：贝克曼夫妇（Anna-Lisa and Sven-Eric Beckeman）

（图片提供：Spink China）

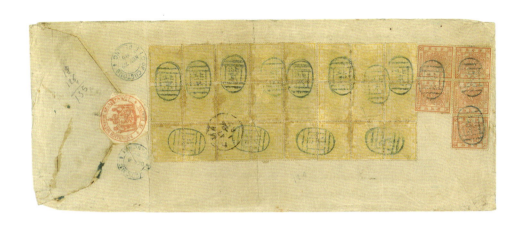

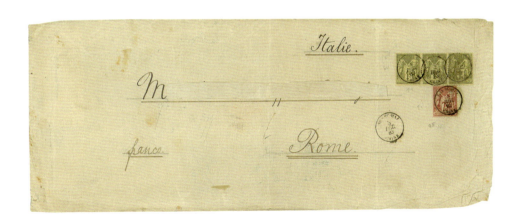

1885 年 8 月 7 日镇江寄美国封

1885 年 8 月 7 日，镇江寄美国纽约（New York）。

正面：贴 5 分美国邮票，销盖红色杀手戳。另销 1885 年 8 月 7 日镇江海关日戳和 1885 年 8 月 9 日上海美国客邮局红色日戳。

背面：贴大龙厚纸叁分银一枚，销盖 1885 年 8 月 7 日镇江海关日戳。另销 1885 年 8 月 8 日上海海关日戳、1885 年 9 月 3 日旧金山红色日戳和 1885 年 9 月 10 日纽约日戳。

源流：贝克曼夫妇（Anna-Lisa and Sven-Eric Beckeman）、林文琰（Lam Man Yin）、丁劲松（Ding Jin Song）

（图片提供：丁劲松先生）

1886 年 10 月 5 日天津寄丹麦封

1886 年 10 月 5 日，天津寄丹麦哥本哈根（Copenhagen）。

正面：贴法国客邮 25 生丁两枚，销盖 1886 年 10 月 13 日上海法国客邮局日戳。另销天津海关椭圆挂号戳和上海法国客邮局红色方形挂号戳。

背面：贴大龙厚纸叁分银横四连和壹分银横三连，销盖天津海关黑色椭圆中文戳和挂号戳。另销 1886 年 10 月 5 日天津海关日戳、1886 年 10 月 9 日上海海关日戳、1886 年 10 月 17 日法国轮船邮局戳、1886 年 11 月 18 日巴黎日戳和 1886 年 11 月 20 日丹麦哥本哈根日戳。

源流：龚文生（Wen Sun Kong）、龚秀彬（Robert S.P. Kong）

（图片提供：Interasia Auctions）

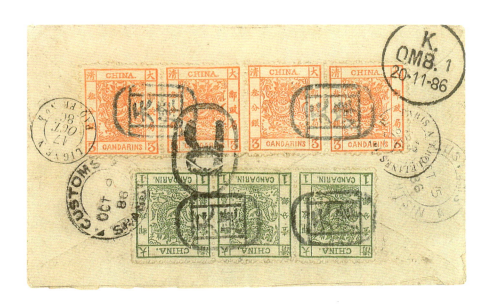

1887 年 5 月 18 日镇江寄丹麦封

1887 年 5 月 18 日，镇江寄丹麦哥本哈根（Copenhagen）。

正面：贴 25 生丁法国邮票，销盖 1887 年 5 月 20 日上海法国客邮局日戳。

背面：贴大龙厚纸伍分银和小龙壹分银、叁分银各一枚，销 1887 年 5 月 18 日镇江海关日戳。另销 1887 年 5 月 19 日上海海关日戳、1887 年 5 月 24 日法国轮船邮局日戳和 1887 年 6 月 29 日哥本哈根日戳。

源流：林文琰（Lam Man Yin）、丁劲松（Ding Jin Song）

（图片提供：丁劲松先生）

鸣　谢

英国邮政博物馆的马特·谭托里（Matt Tantony）先生和海伦·狄叶特（Helen Dafter）女士、大英图书馆的保罗·斯金纳（Paul Skinner）先生和理查德·莫雷尔（Richard Morel）先生，以及德纳罗公司的萨尔塞多·乔吉（Salzedo Georgie）先生为资料的搜寻查阅提供了极大的便利。

本书在原始档案辨识、翻译过程中得到杰弗里·S. 舒耐特（Jeffrey S. Schneider）博士、朱逢华（Edward Chu）博士、张兰青先生和黄嘉宝（Cecilia Vong）小姐的大力支持。

朱逢华博士、罗伯特·舒耐特（Robert Schneider）先生为本书的序言英译彻夜劳心。

丁劲松先生、孙吉博士、赵建先生和陈拓雄先生，保利国际、香港国际亚洲（Interasia Auctions）、斯宾客（Spink China）和苏富比/科林菲娜（Sotheby's and Corinphila）等拍卖公司为本书提供了珍贵的图片。

徐贞小姐为此书的最终完稿投入了颇多的时间和精力，曹海艳小姐和李卓小姐在档案的收集整理过程中亦付出了辛勤的汗水。

李曙光将军在成书过程中给予了特别的关心和指导。

潘振平先生自资料整理之初，即给予此项研究方向性指导，完稿过程之中亦耗费心血逐字逐句进行译文校核，同时还拨冗撰序进行研究论述。

陆智昌先生装帧设计的生花妙笔，以及中华书局罗华彤老师审读校阅的细致周全，让我感慨良深。

在此谨向他们表示由衷的谢意。

参考文献

[1] 沈云龙. 近代中国史料丛刊第六十二辑：筹办夷务始末（同治朝）[G]. 台北：文海出版社，1966.

[2] （台北）"交通部邮政总局". 大龙邮票封戳选辑 [M].1978.

[3] 中国近代经济史资料丛刊编辑委员会. 中国海关与邮政 [M]. 北京：中华书局，1983.

[4] 集邮编辑部. 集邮 [J]. 北京：中国集邮出版社，1988(10).

[5] 梁鸿贵. 大龙邮票纪念专集——纪念大龙邮票发行 110 周年 1878—1988[C]. 北京：中国集邮出版社，1988.

[6] 八〇二邮友俱乐部. 谭邮四周年纪念——大龙邮票汇探心得 [J].1988.

[7] 仇润喜. 天津邮政史料（第一辑）[M]. 北京：北京航空学院出版社，1988.

[8] 刘肇宁. 大龙邮票 [M]. 北京：科学普及出版社，1988.

[9] 天津市档案馆，中国集邮出版社. 清末天津海关邮政档案选编 [G]. 许和平，张俊桓，译. 北京：中国集邮出版社，1988.

[10] 中国邮票博物馆. 大龙邮票与清代邮史 [M]. 香港：商务印书馆（香港）有限公司，北京：故宫博物院紫禁城出版社，1989.

[11] 陈霞飞. 中国海关密档——赫德、金登干函电汇编（1874—1907）[G]. 北京：中华书局，1990—1996.

[12] 费拉尔手稿——清代邮政邮票和明信片备忘录 [G]. 北京：人民邮电出版社，1991.

[13] 黄建斌. 大龙邮票集锦 1878—1885 [M].1993.

[14] 范慕韩. 中国印刷近代史（初稿）[M]. 北京：印刷工业出版社，1995.

[15] 黄建斌. 大龙信封存世考 [M]. 台北：财团法人黄建斌文教基金会，1997.

[16] 马传德，徐渊. 揭开"中外通宝"银币之谜 [J]. 中国钱币，1997(4).

[17] 天津市邮电管理局，中华全国集邮联合会. 纪念大龙邮票发行 120 周年集邮学术研讨会论文汇编 [C].1998.

[18] 中华人民共和国信息产业部《中国邮票史》编审委员会.中国邮票史(第一卷)[M].
北京：商务印书馆，1999.

[19] 王宏斌.赫德爵士传——大清海关洋总管 [M].北京：文化艺术出版社，2000.

[20] 陈升贵.北京工业志·印刷志 [M].北京：中国科学技术出版社，2001.

[21] 中国海关学会.赫德于旧中国海关论文选 [C].北京：中国海关出版社，2004.

[22] 理查德·J·司马富，约翰·K·费正清，凯瑟琳·F·布鲁纳.赫德与中国早期现代化——
赫德日记（1863—1866）[M].陈绛，译.北京：海关出版社，2005.

[23] 万启盈.中国近代印刷工业史 [M].上海：上海人民出版社，2012.

[24] 钱爱德.中国币图说汇考——金银镍铝 [M].钱屿，钱卫，译.北京：金城出版社，
2014.

[25] 孙浩.百年银圆 [M].上海：上海科学技术出版社，2016.

[26] The Royal Philatelic Society London. *The London Philatelist*[J]. 1903—2018.

[27] The China Stamp Society. *The China Clipper*[J]. 1936—2018.

[28] Easton J. *The DE LA RUE HISTORY of BRITISH & FOREIGN POSTAGE STAMPS, 1855 to 1901*[M]. London: Faber and Faber, 1958.

[29] Fairbank J K, Bruner K F and Matheson E M. *THE I.G. IN PEKING: Letters of Robert Hart, Chinese Maritime Customs, 1868 —1907*[M]. Cambridge, Massachusetts and London: The Belknap Press of Harvard University Press, 1975.

[30] Ireland P W. *CHINA——The Large Dragons 1878 —1885*[M]. London: Robson Lowe Ltd., 1978.

[31] Chen Xiafei and Han Rongfang. *Archives of China's Imperial Maritime Customs: Confidential Correspondence between Robert Hart and James Duncan Campbell, 1874 —1907*[M]. Beijing: Foreign Languages Press, 1990—1993.

[32] Pratt R. *Imperial China——History of the Posts to 1896*[M]. London: Christie's Robson Lowe, 1994.

[33] Pugh P. *The Highest Perfection——A History of De La Rue*[M]. London: Icon Books Ltd., 2011.

[34] Walton F. *The De La Rue Collection*[M]. London: The Royal Philatelic Society, 2014.

拍卖文献

[1] Philippe Renotière de Ferrary, *Gilbert*（Paris），Sale XII, 22-24 April 1925.

[2] Authur Hind, *H.R. Harmer*（New York），20-21 May 1935.

[3] E.H. Finegan, *Harmer Rooke*（London），14-15 October 1937.

[4] George Scudder, *H.R. Harmer*（New York），22 June 1943.

[5] Dr. Warren G. Attwood, *Harmer Rooke*（New York），7-8 October 1952.

[6] H.B.R. Clarke, *Robson Lowe*（London），22 April 1953.

[7] Adolphous Diercking, *H.R. Harmer*（London），5-6 November 1956.

[8] Michael Newbury, *Robert A. Siegel*（New York），6-7 February 1962.

[9] Sir David Roseway, *Robson Lowe*（London），12-13 November 1963.

[10] Robert C.H. Lee, *J.R. Hughes*（San Francisco），16 November 1963 and 29 February 1964.

[11] Sir Percival David, *Robson Lowe*（London and Basel），18 September 1963, 16 December 1964, 4 October 1967, 13 November 1969, 22 July 1970, 26 October 1970, 20 March 1975.

[12] C.F. Gordon, *Robson Lowe*（London），21 April 1964.

[13] Godfrey Mellor, *Robson Lowe*（London），15 May 1969.

[14] Dr. Warren G. Kauder, *Robson Lowe*（London），10 November 1971 and 2-4 May 1972.

[15] Richard Canman, *Stanley Gibbons*（London），19-20 October 1972.

[16] Lyons F. Livingston, *H.R. Harmer*（New York），4-5 December 1973.

[17] Paul Hock, *Robson Lowe*（Zurich），19 October 1983.

[18] Giulio Mochi, *David Feldman*（Zurich），24 October 1984.

[19] *Corinphila*（Zurich），25 March 1987 and 29 September 1988.

[20] Bernard Stoloff, *Christie's Robson Lowe*（Zurich），14 May 1987.

[21] Philip W. Ireland, *Christie's Robson Lowe*（Zurich），25 May 1989.

[22] Major James Starr, *Sotheby's*（London），11-13 September 1991.

[23] Henry Everall, *Stanley Gibbons*（Australia），20 February 1993.

[24] James B.Whang, *Christie's Swire*（Hong Kong），2 November 1994.

[25] Anna-Lisa and Sven-Eric Beckeman, *Sotheby's and Corinphila*（Hong Kong），
7 November 1996, 15 May 1997, 7 October 1997.

[26] M. F. Huang, *Zurich Asia*（Hong Kong），21 June 2003.

[27] Jane and Dan Sten Olsson, *Zurich Asia*（Hong Kong），2006.

[28] Meiso Mizuhara, *Spink*（London），17 January 2016.

图书在版编目（CIP）数据

德纳罗密档：1877年中国海关筹印邮票之秘辛/
赵岳译著. -- 北京：中华书局, 2018.7
ISBN 978-7-101-13259-5

Ⅰ.德… Ⅱ.赵… Ⅲ.邮票—历史—中国—清后期
Ⅳ.①F632.9

中国版本图书馆CIP数据核字(2018)第111828号

书　　名	德纳罗密档——1877年中国海关筹印邮票之秘辛	
译 著 者	赵　岳	
装帧设计	陆智昌	
责任编辑	罗华彤	
出版发行	中华书局	
	（北京市丰台区太平桥西里38号　100073）	
	http://www.zhbc.com.cn	
	E-mail:zhbc@zhbc.com.cn	
印　　刷	北京雅昌艺术印刷有限公司	
版　　次	2018年7月北京第1版	
	2018年7月北京第1次印刷	
规　　格	开本/ 787×1092毫米　1/16	
	印张29　字数300千字	
印　　数	1—2500册	
国际书号	ISBN 978-7-101-13259-5	
定　　价	256元